Biography: Judith Gait

Judith Gait studied for her first degree at the California College of Arts and Crafts and for her Master's degree came to Oxford University studying Fine Art at the Ruskin School of Drawing. She is profiled in Who's Who in Art, World Who's Who of Women and the Dictionary of International Biography. Her work is in public and private collections in this country and abroad. She is a 'Star' award finalist for her teaching, particularly those with challenging behaviour and enduring health needs. She also served on the board of one of the largest Mental Health NHS Trusts in the country as a non-executive director for four years. ∎

Artists' Statement

"...I set before you life or death, blessing or curse. Choose life, then, so that you and your descendants may live in the love of the Lord your God, obeying his voice, clinging to him; for in this your life consists..."

Deuteronomy 30:15

"It was you who created my being,
knit me together in my mother's womb.
I thank you for the wonder of my being,
for the wonders of all your creation.

Already you knew my soul;
my body held no secret from you
when I was being fashioned in secret
and moulded in the depths of the earth."

Psalm 138 part 2

"People were bringing little children to him; for him to touch them. The disciples turned them away, but when Jesus saw this he was indignant and said to them, 'Let the little children come to me; do not stop them; for it is to such as these that the kingdom of God belongs.'"

Mark 10:13-15

ARTISTS' STATEMENT

The artwork in these Meditations springs from our belief in these wonderful and healing texts. From its earliest developmental stages, the few hundred cell divisions of the fertilized egg, or blastula, evidence the integrity and direction of creation. From its first moments, life has structure and follows a developmental trajectory which needs only time for fruition. Time is each person's inviolable right.

Some may argue that the words and artworks used here will only re-open old wounds for any couple whose child has been aborted. The subject is better left forgotten, put out of mind. However, when you read the words of the grieving father in these pages, you notice this has not been his experience. Over time the past re-focuses into a sharper image and the pain through an iterative process of silence, guilt and remorse has not abated. We feel this is the case for many. It is only through facing with courage and truth what has happened in the past that any process of healing or inner peace can be attempted. We sincerely hope that people reading these pages will begin a process to inner clarity. Ultimately this book has been put together in an effort to save human life, not to condemn it.

In closing a brief thought from Mother Teresa: children lost through an abortion love their parents, pray for them and forgive them. We also like to think that in some special unfathomable way their souls are resting in the arms of Christ's Mother, who welcomes these children into eternity and gives them the time their parents didn't have. ∎

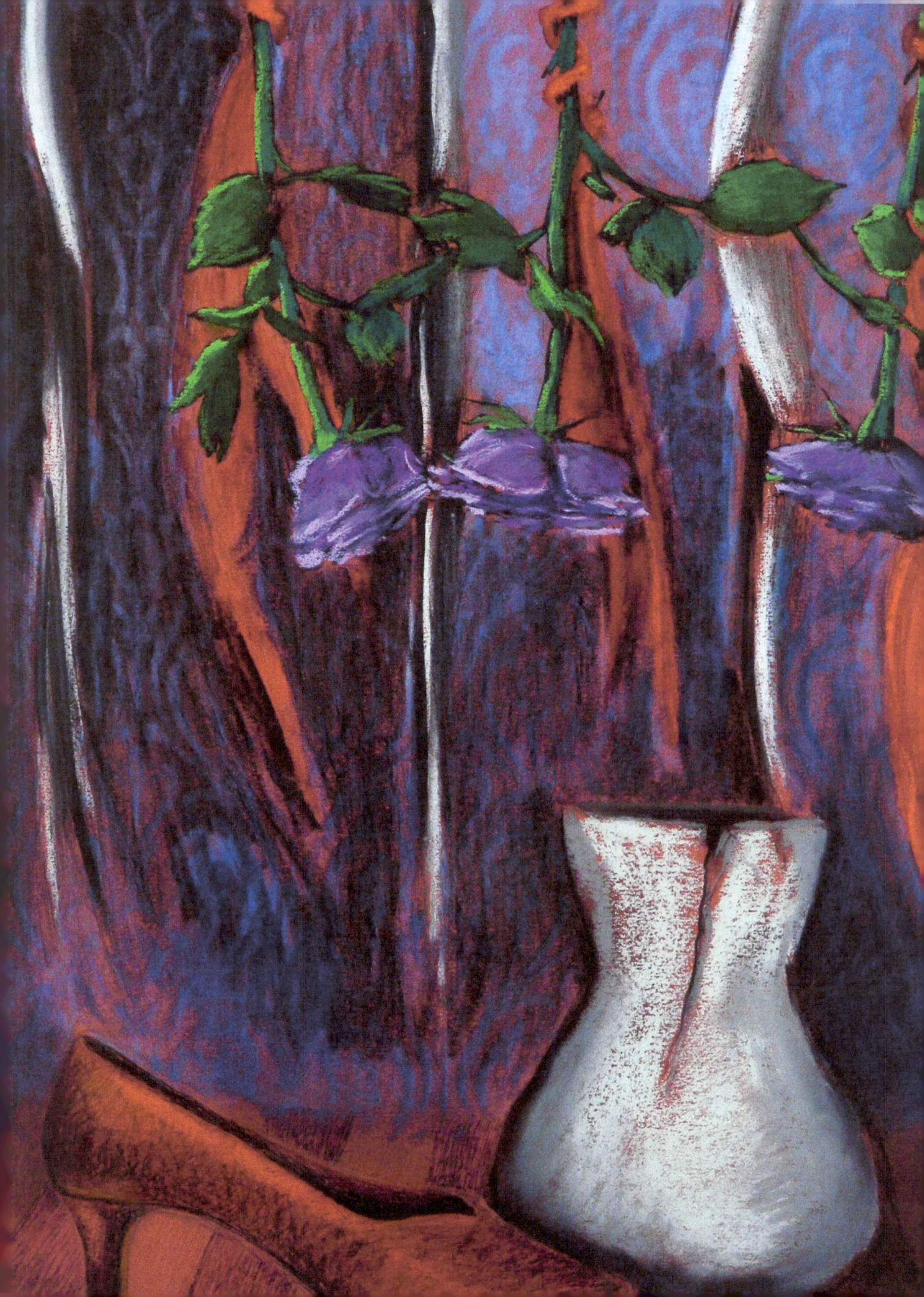

How it all began

letter from Father X to Judith Gait

Dear Judith,

Thank you for the nice cup of tea and chat yesterday. It was a pleasure to visit your lovely village. I enjoyed seeing your studio and viewing your current work still on the drawing board and learning something of the thought and planning that must go into producing a piece of art. I was also very interested in your painting exploring the issues of abortion and particularly when you explained the meaning of the feminine symbols. It was very relevant to me having been touched by this sad experience several years ago. Your ability to place such emotions onto canvas is a gift, such feelings mostly hidden inside and difficult to put into words, your symbols touched me and gave form to my emotion, and therefore have a language of their own. I realise your work comes from a place of great love, for it attempts to give defenceless life the dignity and protection it never knew in our throw away culture. For the parent it stirs up an instinct of longing for that tear drop shaped foetus, which sadly will always be a spirit in limbo and some memory of what might have been. Art like yours also allows for Mother Earth to grieve, to burst forth onto canvas; the use of entangled roses on a vine growing downwards instead of upwards towards the light, the flowers which should be a thing of beauty are finding only increasing shadow; they begin to wither and so the inherent confusion is set up in the painting as sorrow pervades the canvas and in turn nature is thrown off course. The sombreness of this subject is reminiscent of an after the battle scene, some Waterloo of the mind, the single blood red stiletto shoe is the most powerful symbol of termination, and, also the still life of the female form, cut in two, resemble an abstract slaughter house. The brooding wilderness envisaged by T.S. Eliot is present as the painting is drawn inwards by the lack of light, but is redeemed by the power of imagination as a single tree stands

HOW IT ALL BEGAN

like Avalone, symbolising the crown of thorns of Christ, bearing witness to the suffering inherent in this world; a world in which we can still choose to love or not to love. The artist's own deep shout of life and therefore of love is in the painting too; it transcends the clinical act to the abortionist and the art itself becomes a platform for mother and child and the Spirit of forgiveness to grow, and hopefully inspire others who will gaze on this picture or at least reflect more on what is in fact a major life decision: whether to terminate a child or not. Decisions which are often made in fear and confusion and yet usually are paid for in a lifetime of regret. These are paintings which need to be seen and thought about. They enter into an area of life full of public controversy and strong emotion but ultimately too this story is always a very personal journey, usually of a lone female and possibly her lover; if it makes one of them stop and think for a moment or two, all to the good. These works of Art manage to mix the tragedy of life and transcendental love together, and still deal with the thorny issue of abortion head on but through an artist's eyes. It is also a work of heartfelt meditation and a silent prayer of witness for all the ghost families, those Phantoms of Sorrows, who never will laugh or cry together as a family, because of an abortion. They just never made it to the starting block of love, the real love of creating and sustaining life. And that is a tragedy!

Troubadours Sailing Hibiscus Seas

MEDITATIONS AND ARTWORK OF POST ABORTION TRAUMA

TARGET BLASTULA

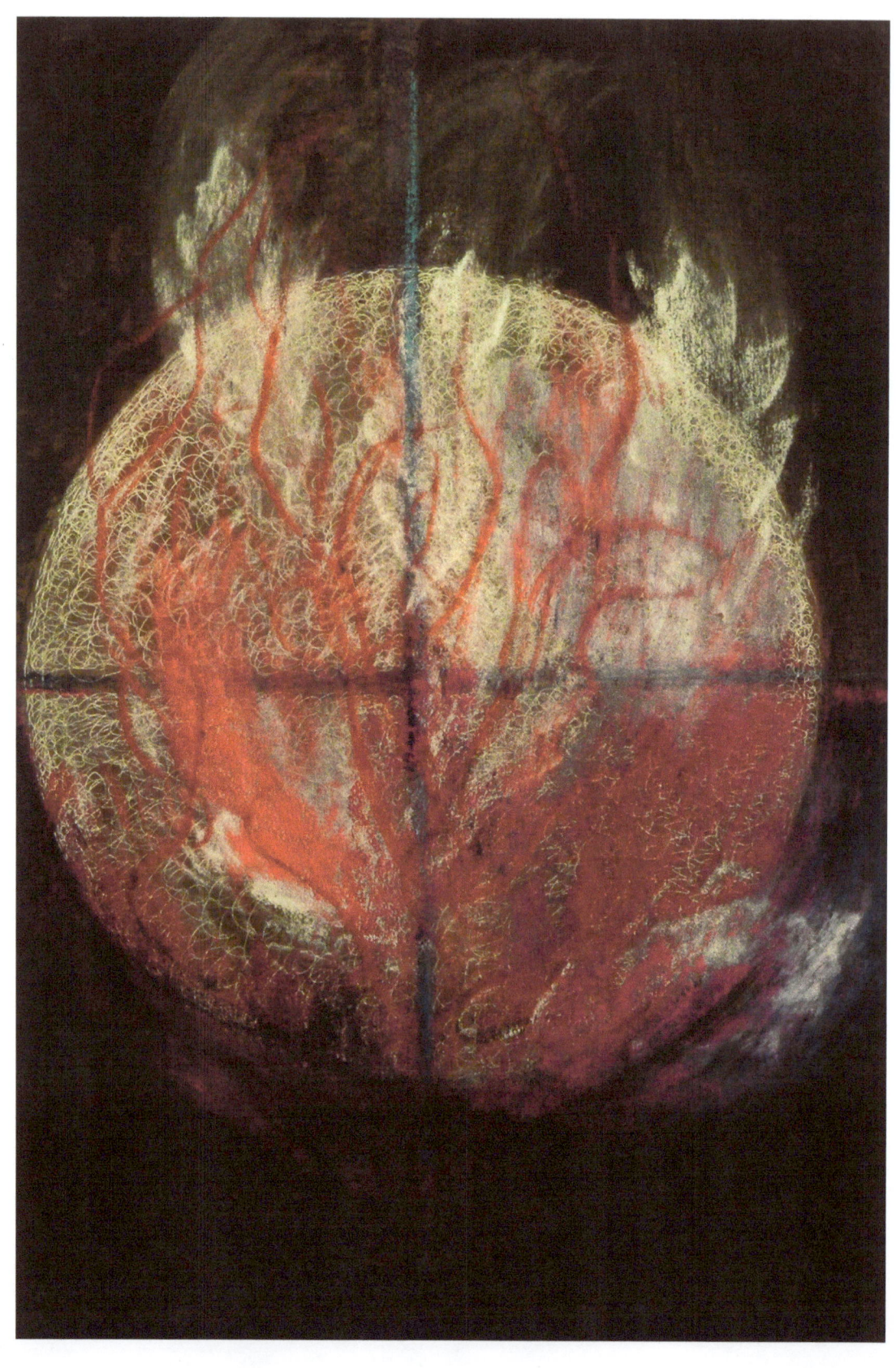

13
TARGET BLASTULA

In the Palm of the Almighty, moulded in the fire of creation, protected by unwritten law and made long before the Word was breathed into the clay of Adam and Eve, I whispered your Patronymic and you heard my name. "Do no harm and know that I am God." Shining stars shimmering just for you, my little love. For somewhere above the starry plough and far away in the celestial galaxy, I am making a home for you. Sinew and sand, molten laver, blood fire flowing free, is the very same workings of the foaming planets forming now in you. They say you are guarded from above and in my Holy Name you are protected by angels. For angels know and angels tell that no baby's cry or butterfly sheen can stir a beating wing without its ripple being felt across the fathomless void. Abortion Law: creation upended. My love for you is in the crosshairs. The battle lines are drawn; Mephistopheles and Christ are rolled up together in an unholy fight for good and evil lie side by side as they go head to head. Mother Mary, speak my name and bring forth the new life destined at your Milken Breast. For in you the opposites converge and in the fire of mystery, my revelation, I reveal to you my true face. ■

JONAH OF NINEVEH

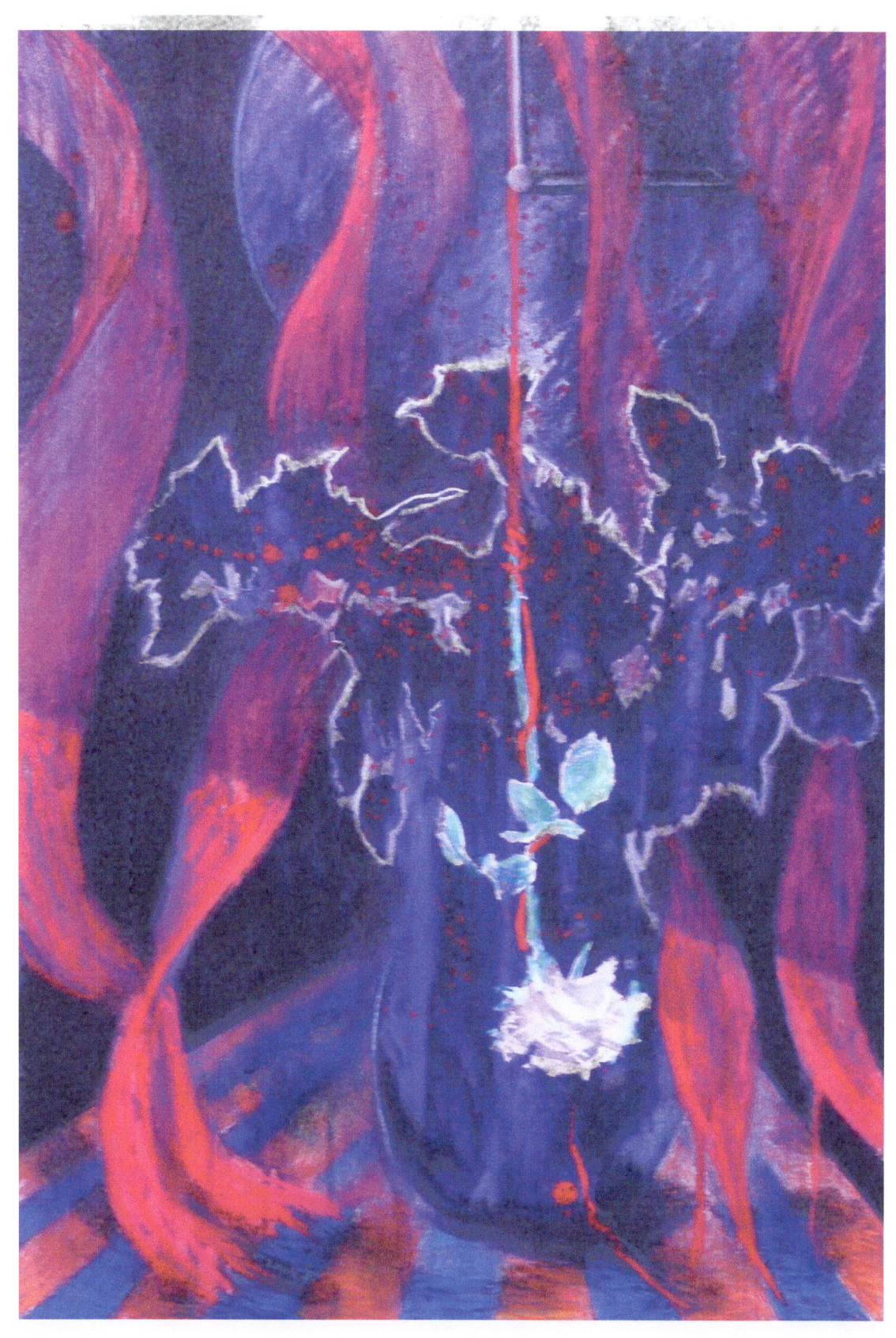

JONAH OF NINEVEH

The seed of life is healthy and strong and sleeps within the mother's womb. It rests in golden slumbers through the gestation period and in this time of formation it is very close to the Lord our God. Baby Mother too dreams her dreams and is visited nightly by angels of the Lord as she is anointed and prepared for the full spectrum of motherhood ahead of those days filled with both hardship and love. While Father dear is preparing with pride or running a mile to make room in his heart for his darling bud to arrive, every child of creation needs loving parents to make it grow.

Jonah fled from parental responsibility away to sea and afterwards a huge storm erupted. The sailors, fearing the hurricane was Jonah's fault, tossed him overboard and the storm abated. Jonah was swallowed whole by a whale and there he remained for three days and three nights. He prayed to the Lord his God with all his might to release him from the belly of the great mammal. Afterwards the Lord relented and Jonah escaped on a spout of water and returned to Nineveh and persuaded the wayward residents to repent. Afterwards Jonah was rewarded with a place in the shade and the ways of a God directed life.

A Pre Redemption Jonah still lives on in seafaring folklore and to be considered a Jonah is to be thought the bearer of bad luck on board ship. Joseph Conrad took us into the Heart of Darkness, exploring the dark forces latent within human beings. In our shadow side is a menagerie of darker forces where "Psycho Killer" meets "American Velvet". Darkness lurks just beneath the surface in all of us; we need God's all redeeming love to guide us or we will surely meet the real stuff of nightmares in our lives.

It was her wedding white dress, my sea green empress, this blue lagoon princess she slipped into her own heart of darkness on that day she decided to abort and when time really stopped in our lives. She was full of fear of the future and without the treasure of wisdom to guide her she chose the path of least resistance or so it seemed at the time.

The love affair was intense but hardly begun, the togetherness and tenderness we felt were all there and on the crest; it was not yet clear whether it would grow into a really strong relationship and last for years or it would die naturally on the vine over time. Fate took a hand and largely because of fear and insecurity on her part the expected congratulations of expectant new life suddenly turned into commiserations of sadness and mistaken folly.

So long as you waver like Jonah in the face of responsibility and lack both the fortitude and faith of a mother and father to do what is right for their child, you will be offered an abortion by a well meaning doctor from the NHS, and, without too much trouble either or so much as a by your leave. Jack Kerouac, the famous American beatnik poet, was correct when he noticed on his road trip, on route 66, the red brick behind every neon sign.

A living, breathing clay jar of a womb is a light to the world, carrying a baby inside. Every picture tells a story and this birthday of a child may not happen as the womb is encroached by the shedding of darkness spreading over its little baby home, as the flowers behind the baby slowly wither and die. The decision is a real crossroads in a woman's life: either continue to germinate and carry a child for a full nine months or terminate before twenty-four weeks are up. The early term weeks of pregnancy have become something of a commodity for medical companies. Medics in white coats are waiting in the wings to offer abortions, a latter day contraceptive bayonet. All of this in the face of a woman's natural instinct and life cycle of motherhood. Bad decisions last a lifetime but someone by then will have taken the money and run.

The central theme of the picture is the deep blue vase. A clay jar would usually be used in the days of Jonah to store and carry water. Latterly it is now used to display flowers, those things of real beauty which are simply glimpses into eternity and what is promised to us all beyond the shadows. The flowers are a cymbal of life and of the womb. The flowers are in darkness and only one flower is in focus and in natural colour. It represents the child who is already in the birth position, head down and waiting to be born. The baby does not know it is trapped in a life and death struggle of motherhood and of waiting on Jonah who is busy running away from fatherhood and now, finding himself trapped in the belly of a Whale, is praying hard for a second chance that might not come again. We ask ourselves, 'will the baby push out naturally and so be allowed to live through a mother's grace to enjoy a proper birthday?'. Or will it be abandoned by its parents to die and be surgically removed from its mother by strangers with forceps; given its own death-day written up as a statistic without a name only to be remembered each year by two forlorn and guilty parents?

The spirals represent the veil that separates the two worlds of the living and the dead. The spirals represent the DNA helix of the child and the veil of the Temple which has just been rudely shaken to its foundations. The clock in the background marks the point of death when time stood still for the parents and for the heavens above. Each child's death shakes the Temple of the Lord as one more innocent victim is taken from this world to the next one beyond. And every human being that remains on this earth is lessened as a result. For we did nothing like enough to save an aborted child and so a little bit of our own humanity dies along with the little terminated foetus. ∎

HAMMER OF DECISION

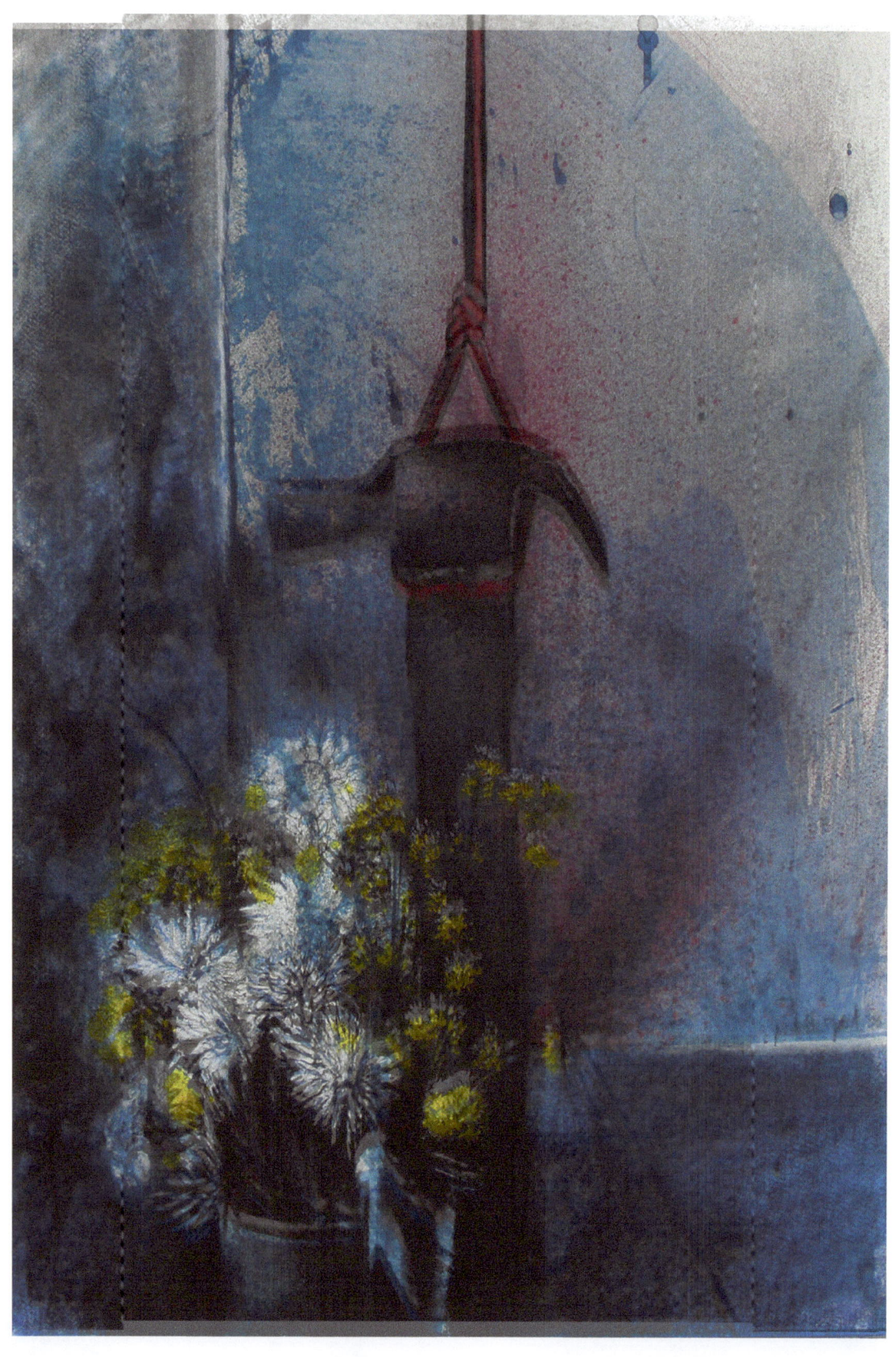

HAMMER OF DECISION

The Ring of the Nibelung, which includes the 'March of the Valkyries', is made famous in popular culture by Francis Ford Coppola's film, 'Apocalypse Now'; it is the soundtrack to US Army helicopters attacking and bombing a Vietnamese village. The Valkyries were warrior women who married husbands destined to die in battle shortly after matrimony. The Valkyries would then escort their late husbands to Valhalla. The epic story of Nibelung is based on Northern European mythology and follows the lives of the Nordic Gods; written over 20 years by Richard Wagner in four classic operas known as the Ring cycles. In old Norse mythology Thor is the Nordic hammer God of war who falls under the spell of Woden, the one eyed God who exchanged his eye for Power. Under Woden's influence Thor destroyed his enemies with a reign of hammer blows and intrigue.

With time things change and in Europe the Church made its presence felt everywhere. Instead of hammer war we see a law of hammer wisdom. Joseph the Carpenter and husband of Mary. Yusef believes in the One true God of Abraham, and is made the patron saint of workers by mother church. Joseph's workforce is a world away from Thor. They are devoted to creation and they value children as gifts of heaven. These parents of labour who gather together in the workplace of schools and crèche to hammer into shape beautiful things in order for children to grow up feeling safe and secure. This world made up of love for children is the family home, made through self sacrifice and hard work: a utopia of love as foretold by Thomas More. They built mother ships and submarines with babies' wings to explore new worlds of being and they brought back home the Empires of the Son.

It is very symbolic that a hammer is used as a centre piece of decision making for abortion. The hammer of decision represents the outcome of female contemplation. A baby will either receive a death of a thousand cuts or it will be fashioned by love through family life.

20
HAMMER OF DECISION

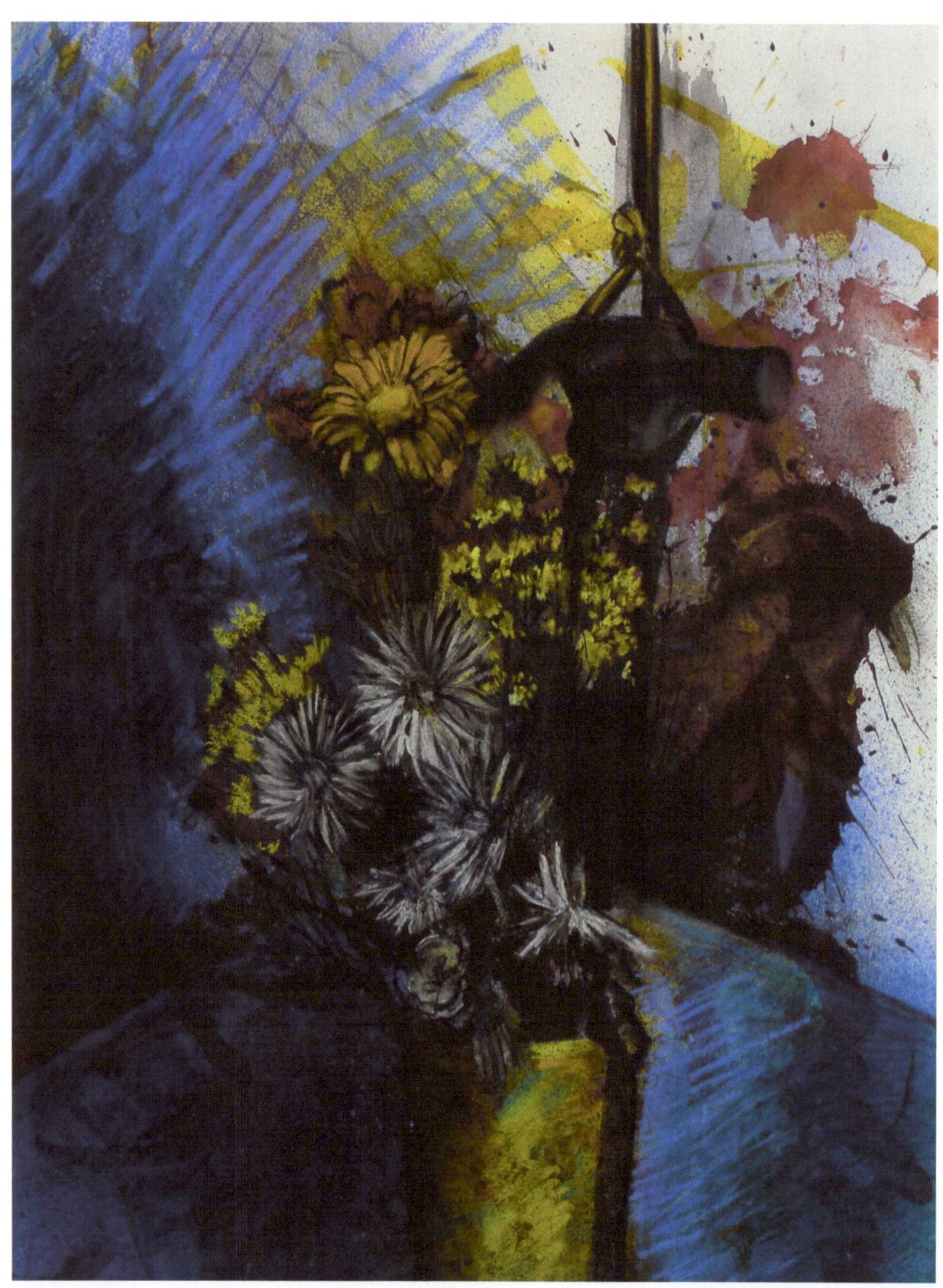

21
HAMMER OF DECISION

The hammer is the symbolic instrument of choice – it will either build a home or tear it down. The decision of termination is final; there are no second chances with an abortion. Only a lost world of forgiveness; a cry for mercy to the lost baby is the only thing to expect next for the parent and transmitted by baby dreams through some distant Sun.

Thor's hammer is a tool of chaos and it wants to tear apart the past, and lay waste to our old traditions and civilizations. The hammer of Thor wants to rule the world and will stop at nothing to get power; will smash up past, present and future. The embryo is the future. The northern war God allied to Woden is infected with his one eyed wisdom of intrigue and destruction. In contrast to Thor, Joseph the worker wants to build families and communities for the purpose of living life and prays daily at the Tabernacle of the Lord. The master carpenter wants to do God's work to set people free to live in peace and social justice.

There is still time left for maidens between the moment of conception and their hammer choice of life or death. The Valkyries - the choosers of the Slain - can also through wisdom be the legion of fighting mothers who will take the high road of Joseph and Mary. The Patron Saint of workers will make a baby's Crib and build a home for a loving wife and family. The Valkyries of Joseph will then expel the message of Thor and his hammer house of horrors and transport him and his hammer to Valhalla.

The Valkyries hold the key to the future. The embryo is alive from the moment of Conception. It is an Olympian role model and has exceptional durability. In the world of competitive sport, sperm racing comes out in a league of its own, with over 270 million contestants present at each jet race of love. But only one tad of sperm can be the winner and get to fertilize the Egg of Life. The Valkyries of Thor who finally choose to abort will take away a little life and spoil the mating game in one bold toilet flush.

HAMMER OF DECISION

The hammer of Thor will disrupt the trans-migration of children's souls, those beings built for love who will make up our next generation. The question remains: will our duty as parents towards tomorrow's world be shouldered or will it not? During love making Mother Nature is summoned by our passion and the spirits of the future hover over the parents waiting for that moment of Conception. When the star bursts and the moment arrives and the two parents are finally joined in fruitful union their cells diverge into new life and a baby is beheld in the eyes of God. Flowers are a symbol of Mother Nature's sons and daughters; that a baby has been conceived and is now the fruit of the womb. The lifeline now begins with the flow of nutrients for the development of brain and bone. The sacred umbilical cord is nature's daisy chain, a thread of life which keeps mother connected and baby alive. The law of creation is now growing a baby and with the maidens' consent our legion of Valkyries will soon be mothers in waiting.

If instead our society views abortion as a mercy killing to protect a woman's rights, is this just a sign of our own moral decline? In the Western world we start wars of conquest and not stopping these wars is an acid test of our real values. The colour revolutions and the monkey law of military interventions are rarely instigated on our own streets to change policy and bring on love and understanding to save our own children-in-law. Where now is the new white man's burden; this so called responsibility to protect; to prevent the killing of innocents? Or is this just another lie in the killing game of psychological warfare? This silence for children's welfare and the lack of deeper knowledge of our role in creation is the art of euthanasia and is a real bonfire of the vanities. The hearts of parents who choose to abort will only harden over time and will open themselves up to the terrible twins of guilt and remorse.

Where is the baby talk of humanitarian intervention? Why are there no human rights violations? Why no calls for a no fly zone overhead; no UN resolutions passed to mandate against fratricide?

HAMMER OF DECISION

Instead we have just a normal everyday medical procedure called an abortion: a Frankenstein operation in reverse. In the West we make our own rope to eventually hang ourselves. We have taken our eye off the Way of Joseph and Mary and surrendered our soul to globalization where everything is measured in pounds, shillings and pence; where we know the price of everything but the value of nothing. We will pay for our moral decline for we are being blinded to the truth by the one eyed wisdom of Woden in accepting and spreading Thor's hammer of war. This battle cry of insanity is now focussed on the unborn, just another hapless victim of the undead who rule over us.

The choice for the Valkyries will make or break a family. For those who refuse to drink from the pool of the future will never know the joy of the next generation. So this challenge and responsibility for raising a family, will it be met and shouldered by parents or will they let their own baby's cry go unheard and squashed to death in an orgy of convenience. You choose?

ROSE HIPS AND THE SEA

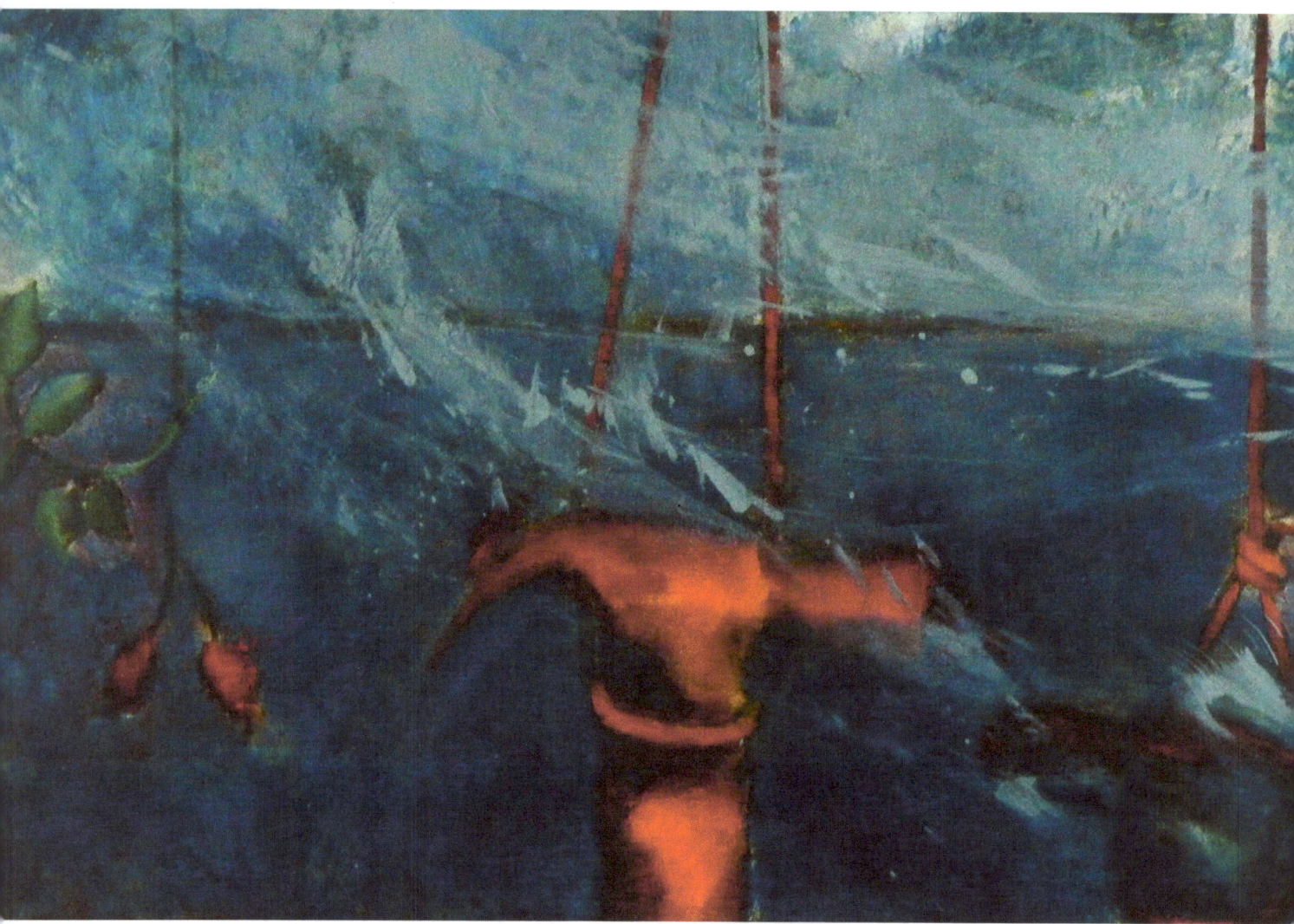

The underwater bloody red hammers represent the irreversible decision to abort a child. The painting captures the action momentarily suspended in time, the viewer is allowed to gaze on a fluid water world scene, the sea of decision. Amongst the striding hammers are the rose pod babies living just beneath the surface of the sea making up their gestation time. They are full of promise for the future but awaiting nonetheless the outcome of the decision whether they will continue to live or will die on demand.

The fluid of the sea is the same element holding the baby in its sack of nibbling yoke. The baby is held in place much like a nautical compass is held in place, buffeted here, there and everywhere as mother rolls this way and that like a big ship of the line bulging her beams out.

The Mother-to-be is increasingly chubby and plump, as she becomes more noticeably with child. Her baby wheels are churning and stretching her Insides out. The baby-headed compass will usually point due South, unless stuck in the breech position. When ready the baby is aimed to shoot out like a lightning bolt fired by a God inspired shot. In the meantime and before the due date, the little baby is just content to rest up close in mummy's fluid belly bath and just keep out of sight in the underwater pod of the deep blue baby sea.

Kicking and screaming like a children's playground fight the twenty four week abortion clock with its claw hammer hands is slowly ticking away on an unborn's life. Tick Tock, tick tock, the baby is in the dock. The judge of foolishness is in his chambers counting out the cost, while mother is in the kitchen eating bread and treacle. The jury is out to lunch and can't make a decision and choose life. Meanwhile the big abortion business is making hay while the sun shines.

A once fertile sea of sweet children's dreams is soon to drown under hammer blows as termination day fast approaches. Tens of thousands of hammers are marching in one direction in the race of no return. Abortion babies who will never know their name only their termination number and a two penny candle to call their own. A candle flame quickly blown out is their only marker of ever having been a sparkle in their father's eye.

Heraclitus the old Greek philosopher once said: 'We cannot step into the same river twice.' The baby steamer sailing on children's seas comes by once a year picking up babies who have been in the fertile sea for nine months growing into someone's son and daughter. These water babies are protected, kept safe and sealed in a pod under the surface of the sea until they are ready to love. They don't have a name yet or even a birth date, but in order for this to happen they must first rise to the surface to begin the process of being harvested by the baby steamer. Then when scooped up from the sea they will be turned over to the Stork who is their sky pilot on their birthday flying them quickly away to their parents' hearts. Then mum and dad will take over and care for their babies forever, in all weather fair or foul, in sickness and in health, richer or poorer and till death do them part.

The hammer of abortion choice is whether or not to give your baby a one way ticket to the stars or take out a round trip with maternity leave. The decision to keep a baby will allow more parents to come aboard the baby steamer making comfortable round trips each year, happily travelling across the baby sweet sea adding to their growing family by accepting more deliveries of children from the Stork and his friends the Pelicans, both together making up the newly born air force of joy.

Peace on the water is needed to make clear headed decisions about keeping babies. Our baby was conceived in the Lake District, an area of outstanding natural beauty and one of the most picturesque areas in England. It was our first proper weekend away together and we stayed at the Nanny Brow, an upmarket hotel near Coniston Water. It was the most perfect weekend in late September, a real Indian summer. With deep blue skies, still clean air and warm, breezing sunshine, a Californian weekend in England. The guest house was perfect and luxurious. We overlooked a craggy fell almost certainly mapped out by the famous Alfred Wainwright, the champion of Lakeland Topography. Outside the window each night was a hooting owl. In the morning a full English breakfast set us up for the day ahead.

The Lakes is also known as Wordsworth country – the famous English Romantic poet lived here. We visited his old house, now a museum, and soaked up the literary beauty of this Cumberland Wordsmith who transformed the countryside into lyrical rolling words filled with beauty inspired from the

ROSE HIPS AND THE SEA

magical surroundings of Fell and mountainscape.

The irony of the weekend in light of what happened next; we visited the home of Beatrix Potter, the famed children's author of such classics as Peter Rabbit and Jemima Puddle-Duck. The glorious weather we had enjoyed up to now broke on this visit and it poured down with rain all day. Another omen.

The day before this downpour we sailed in perfect conditions on Coniston Water on an Italian style Gondola to the home of John Ruskin, the famed Victorian who set up the Ruskin School of Drawing at Oxford University. Ruskin was the most famous art critic of the 19th century and a great humanitarian. His work inspired many social reformers and enlightened pedagogues throughout the world. We also had time to row a boat on Lake Windermere to add to the nautical theme of the weekend. The baby of the deep blue sea was conceived amidst the spirits of all these great souls who went before us in the land of Lakes. We finished off the weekend with a Family Reunion. Another sad irony.

Four weeks later she discovered she was pregnant and at first was delighted and willing to let nature takes its course. What happened next was a tragedy for all three of us and something we both have to live with for the rest of our lives. It may not mean much to others or touch their lives but to me in that moment it was everything and started a lifetime of regret the day she aborted our child. ■

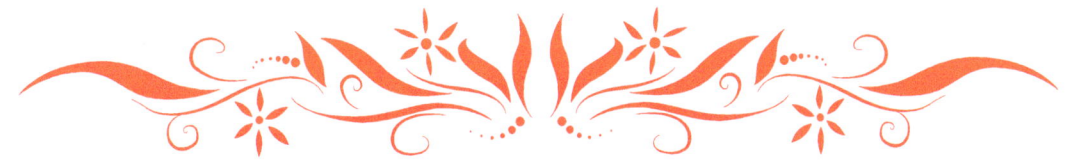

BEARING WITNESS

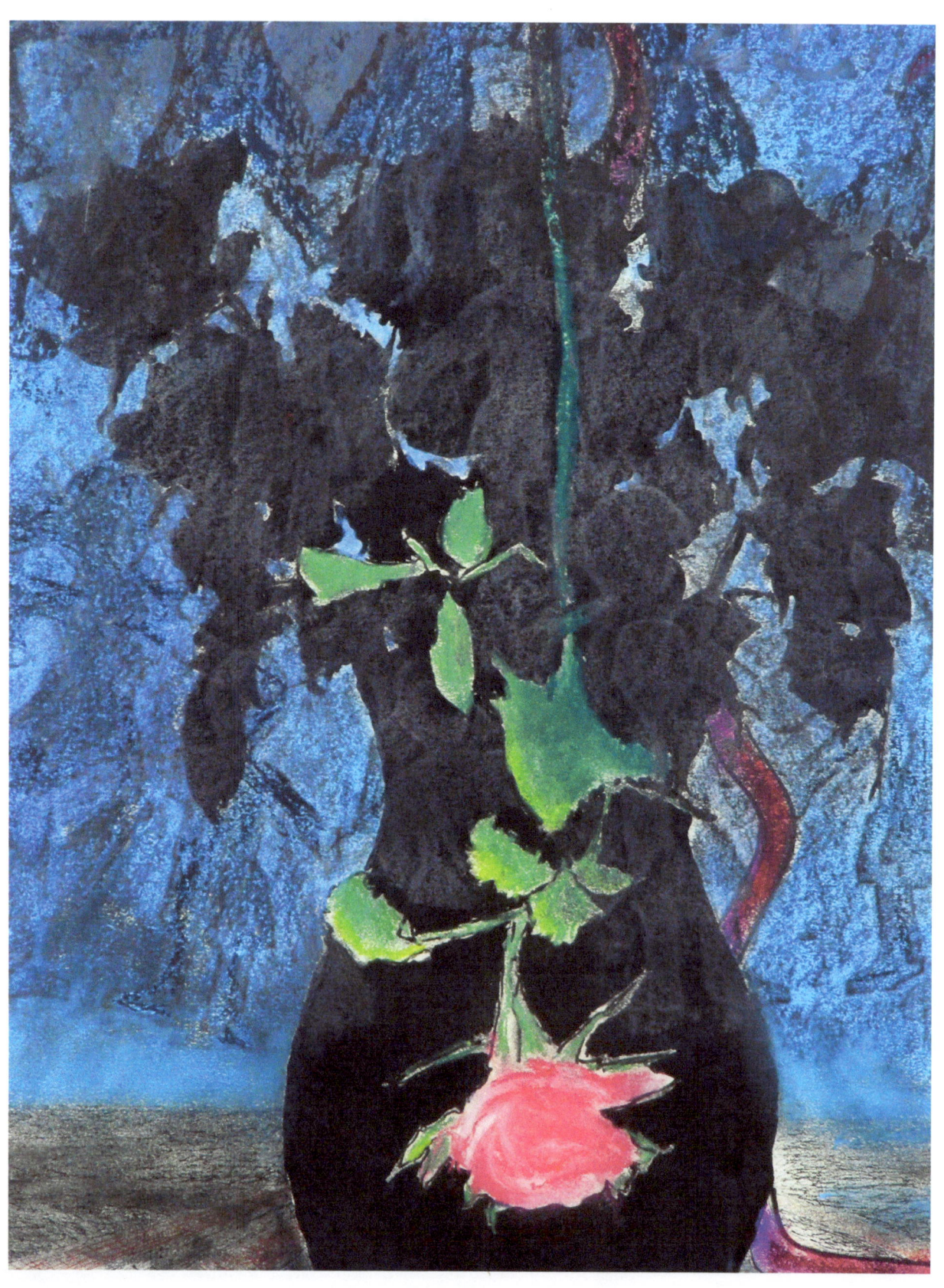

BEARING WITNESS

When a child of the human race is born and is an infant made in the image and likeness of their creator, a new family chapter is written in the book of life. A baby is a product of evolution and a window on the soul of heaven, a blank page, a veritable open book and with it goes clear helplessness: it is a sure heaven sent sign of our dependence on God and on others. From Conception babies need to be loved by their parents and if cherished and allowed to live beyond twenty four weeks after conception will grow up to be responsive adults and have an instinctual desire to want to share the love they have been given with others. Being loved is the soul food that makes children grow up strong in body and mind. When mixed with mother's milk, maternal love is the most nourishing food for young children. Babies have a future ahead of them and they especially need tenderness and cuddles to thrive and become well rounded people. However, if the nurture of mother's love is denied them then babies will wither away and die spiritually as surely as the premeditated prenatal violence of an abortion.

All babies jump for Jesus; each time they give a kick, in their mummy's tummy, they are kicking for him. The baby Jesus was settled in the womb of Mary. He was responsive to God and most loving to the needs of others even when still in the womb. He was so attuned to the needs of others he cried for his brothers and sisters, wanting them to be happy and free. During the Mass we break the bread, to symbolize the value of sharing what we have and we drink his blood to show that sharing what we have is what gives life meaning. The sacrifice of communion is showing the daily willingness we have to give up on selfishness and do God's will and to call on His name to support us in this Action. By participating in communion, a re-enactment of the last supper that Jesus shared with the Twelve Disciples, we too sit at his table and become Good Shepherds and Fishers of Men.

Being homeless in Bethlehem and with no room at the Inn, the first family of Holy Name gave birth to their first child in a stable. Born into a world of space and time Jesus was transcendent, becoming a possible future direction of man representing the capacity we all have for love and transformation.

The baby Jesus was wrapped in swaddling clothes and laid in a crib by Mary and Joseph. He was a symbol of non duality, the unity of opposites. His life pointed the way to the pure mind of the Kingdom of God buried deep down within us. Here the lord of the house, the Jesus place, is speaking to us constantly by giving direction to fulfil His message of love and service. This is our true purpose of being born, to awaken and not be slaves of selfishness.

The cow is a sacred animal – they give much abundance to humanity and they watched over baby Jesus in the Stable. A great star settled overhead, guiding the three wise kings from the East who had followed the new light all the way to Bethlehem. The three gurus brought with them Gold, Frankincense and Myrrh; a needed camouflage due to the constant threat of King Herod's spies and the surveillance of the population by the Empire. The travellers' real gifts were of a spiritual nature, esoteric knowledge for the new born child and his parents confirmed and foretold by the old Testament prophets; that the birth of a child by the sign of the rose would herald in a new Age of Aquarius. The wise men from the East would stay with baby Jesus and oversee his spiritual development from afar until he was twelve when he would travel great distances to be with his teachers and be initiated further into the great mysteries of Heaven and Earth.

The message of Jesus the Saviour was badly needed in the ancient world because the world of Egypt, Greece and Rome was built on slavery, a social system of exploitation which is an affront to God, to human dignity and progress. Jesus would become a great son, prophet and master who taught antiquity to 'love the lord your God with all your heart and thy neighbour as thyself'. This simple egalitarian message, the bread of life, was born, in a Herd-Man's shed in Judah over 2,000 years ago. A concept men have fought over and wrestled within

BEARING WITNESS

themselves over and over ever since. Whether or not to preserve this noble ideal of truth and justice, that finds resonance in noble hearts, in the face of its many evil adversaries, in the dark realms. William Wilberforce and John Brown, now lying in the grave, were inspired by Jesus and went on to move mountains to reach their objective of finally igniting the fire of freedom, setting the slaves free. A slow fuse indeed but one lit by Jesus.

No ornate marble floors or king's ransom at the Saviour's feet; just straw, mud and domesticated animals. The shepherds who watched their flock at night stole away to be beside the crib while angels stood watch over their flocks. The shepherds' lives totally changed after witnessing the sacred birth of Jesus. They went on to inspire and father the Apostles who would spread the message of Christ into the four corners of the ancient world. Even though they and their descendants were hunted by the authorities for the next three hundred years they would not give up. They welcomed martyrdom for Christ and became fishers of men instead of followers of sheep.

A humble carpenter from the line of David, Joseph would apprentice the boy Jesus in carpentry until he was twelve. Mother Mary, the darling bud of May, suckled the baby child with the milk of human kindness and goodness so he could grow in the image and likeness of God.

A mother's love never dies but lives on into eternity from mother to mother; it is an unbroken link with our origins that we were made for love. The thread in the painting symbolises this fact of our lives as it comes from the past and continues off canvas into the future. This is the universal thread of love that connected Mary to Jesus and connects every woman to her child in this golden thread of family life.

Jesus became fully grown in righteousness after a long time spent in contemplation in the desert and after all those years missing from the historical

32
BEARING WITNESS

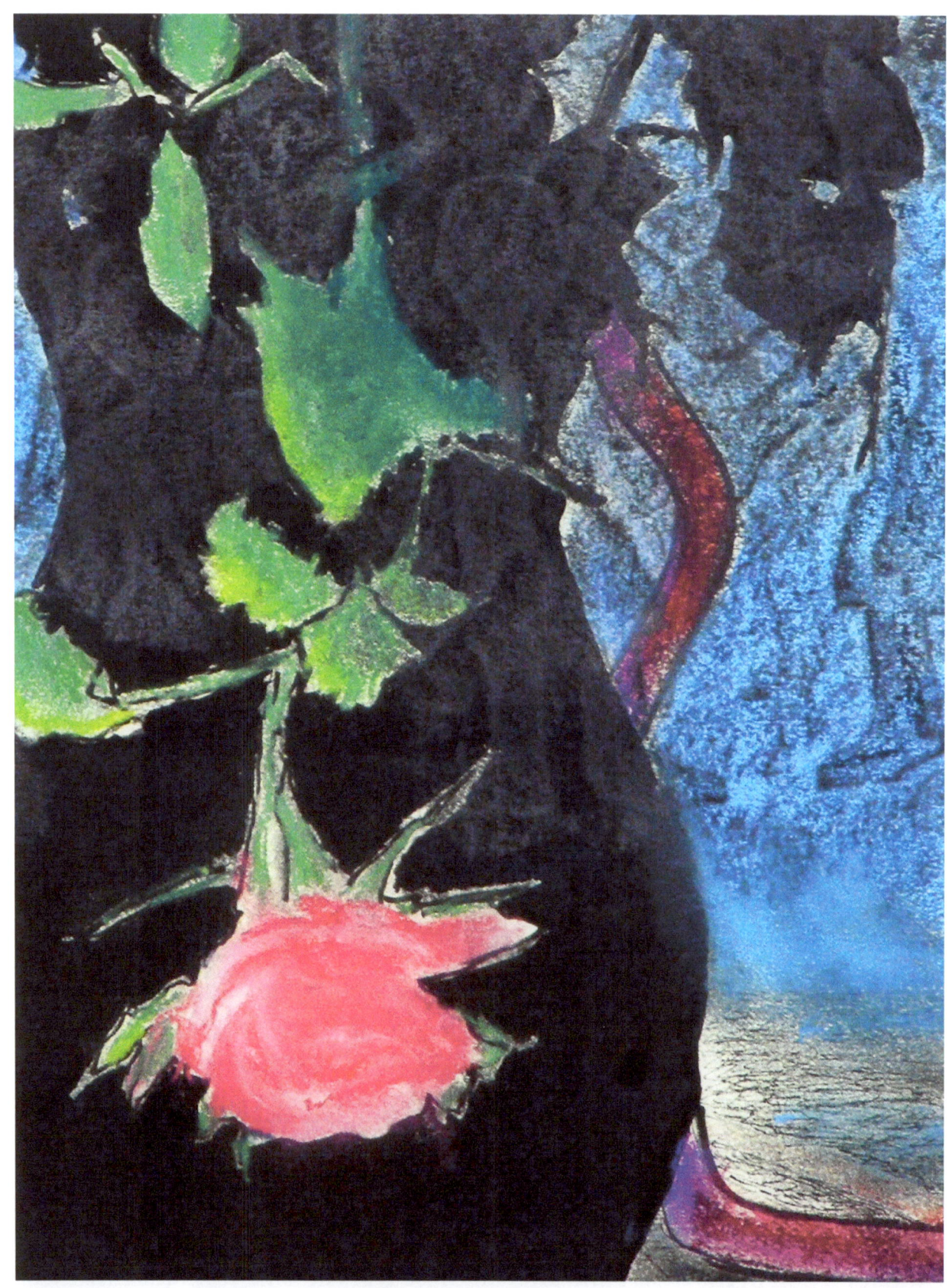

record. Time spent travelling in the East with the three gurus, the Father, the Son and the Holy Spirit, his teachers in esoteric knowledge, he returned home to Nazareth and Judea and was quickly brought to heaven by the Archangel Michael and confirmed in the secrets of heaven by his Heavenly Father, the Lord of Hosts. Jesus, a slow lit fuse, was to change the world by his Love. There was a demonstration of his powers through the practice of miracles meant to reassure doubters and the easily led. He cured the sick and made the lame walk, he raised Lazarus from the dead. His three year ministry before death by crucifixion ushered into the world a new way of being in order that the law would be subject to love in the minds of men. Jesus was a child of destiny and was born amongst men to change them into warriors of truth and justice.

The lowly Shepherds and the Three Kings are symbols; they represent our Intellect and Emotions as we always need both for effective action. These two aspects of our mind knit together in Unity and they knelt at the feet of baby Jesus, the face of revealed truth, and all three aspects of truth anointed this Sepulchre as a place of sanctity and pilgrimage where future believers would want to go to sail on the sea of Galilee and tread on the land where Jesus once walked in ancient times.

Jesus the holy one was destined to die on the cross and he faced his fate with courage and steadfastness and would not give in or betray that which had been ordained from above or give in to the sway and temptations of the devil. Oh what mystery and potential each child contains entrusted into the arms of a woman. The gentle nourishing touch of our female nature, our Sophia with all its divine qualities of nurture and compassion.

Jesus was born into this world and changed it; he became the king of forgiveness and second chances. He came and conquered the world of temptation and sacrificed his life so others would be free to believe in Him and his word and Him who sent him. This king of kings was once a baby born in a stable and needed protection when he was helpless and just potential in the mind of his Father. What protection now for the unborn child? Have we no room in our hearts for them? There are many wanting to be born but instead will be cut out from their mother's womb prematurely.

King Herod represented the entrenched power of the day and was a vassal of Roman overlords; he killed all the new-born boys fearing his rule was undermined by the birth of a swaddling child. Gentle Jesus, meek and mild, the emasculated caricature we are sold of Jesus today, really brought a sword of righteousness, the truth; he cleared the temple of money lenders and extortionate interest payments saddled on the young and the poor. He wrought the Temple in two when he breathed his last up on the cross and brought it crashing down around him, a symbol for selfishness and greed. So Jesus our Lord and saviour, watch over us as we walk this hard road and follow your path to stand up and speak the truth to power that abortion is a crime against God and the unborn child.

The world turns on its axis and hangs on its hinges round and round the globe we go where wheels turn and babies are born. The pitch black cauldron in the painting shaped as a flower vase is a melting pot of formation and creation. The seed inseminates the egg and the chickens come home to roost. Mother Nature takes over after parents have finished with each other and a child is in formation, and judging by the colour and position of the rose a child is soon to be born. The painting of the vase represents a cosmic soup of fermenting life just waiting until the time is ripe to be born.

Jesus was the first born of a new golden era when new law was written in God's love. Before the birth his parents, Mary and Joseph, living under empire obeyed Caesar's law and returned to Bethlehem to be counted in the census. Jesus was a lamb before God but a lion before men. He wore justice on his sleeve and majesty in his manner and showed kindliness to women and children. After

BEARING WITNESS

facing down the Sanhedrin in the Synagogue at age twelve he was forced to flee Jerusalem and head for the East. He spent many years in the Hindu Kush and the High Himalayas and Northern India being initiated in high esoteric teachings. He had a gift of languages and mastered many tongues and their sacred texts. He prepared himself for many long years in contemplation of the ordained task his Father in heaven had set for him to rescue those who would be saved from Self.

Mary, already heavy with child, heard the angels singing suffer all you children unto me. Every baby aborted is a life lost to love. The eighteen years missing from Christ's life before he reappeared at age thirty to preach his three year ministry in the Holy Land can only be explained by his spiritual training under the three wise men, the masters from Asia and the study of sacred scripture in the East Then, finally, in the desert, where he faced his adversary the Serpent whom he met face to face. He withstood the final challenge of evil where the devil offered him riches beyond measure to abandon his mission of bringing light to the Roman Empire and the world. He willingly met his fate on Calvary and was secure in his sacrifice and martyred for his beliefs and his love. Jesus freed himself by long years of study and sacrifice and if we are to share with him in the evolution of the soul, the next great leap for man, then we must do the same as Him. ■

STARDUST

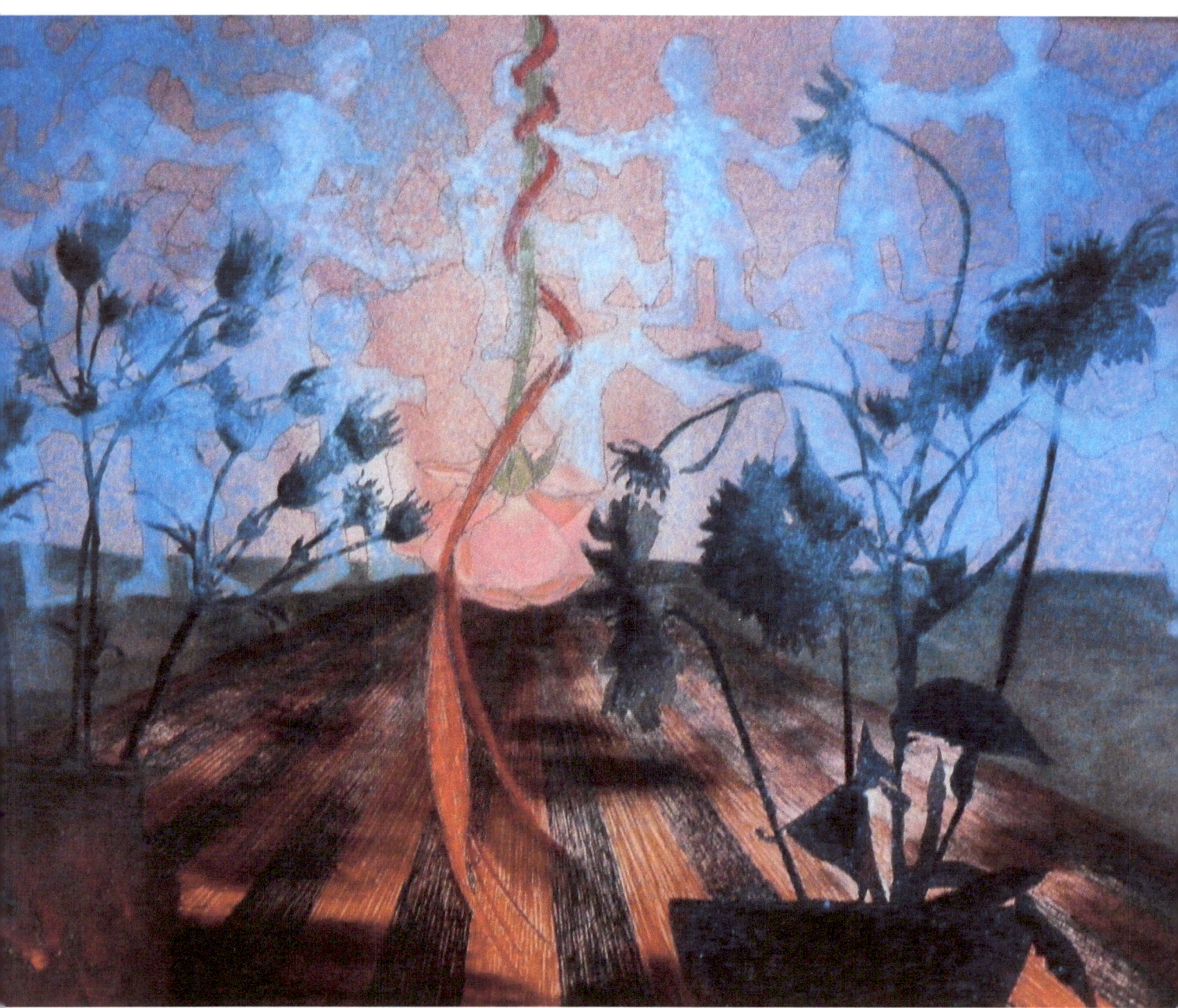

Aborted babies after a termination will take on another trajectory, of spirit. Having been willed into existence by their parents' desire, they must go somewhere after being terminated. In God's kingdom nothing is ever wasted so the partially formed foetus gets recycled by nature and used in some other way to benefit the Universe. The angels' job is to assign the aborted children a new role and it all depends on love.

STARDUST

While the children wait to be loved back to life the angels watch over them. But angels are not parents and in any case angels are always so busy because of so many other terminations. The aborted children stay in holding orphanages and so have lots of free time but they still haven't any parents to fuss over them and send them to school. So they spend their time playing together, all the while waiting to leave the camps and move on to some new form of interplanetary existence.

Meanwhile, in between waiting for their interstellar space trip to begin, they moonlight for the angels. Sometimes the children get to live for a day outside as butterflies, caterpillars, butter-cups and even milk-tops, so hungry Finches and other smaller birds will peck open their lids and drink the cream. In these ways little abortees can be useful to others just like they would have been around the house for mum or dad had they been given an opportunity.

Nonetheless, through being a changeling and without knowing why, they are training themselves for a second chance to be loved because they are learning how to be and how to serve.

Until then the universe and some sensitive and receptive animals have taken them under their wing and are protecting them. Until the day when parents mature, come to their adult senses and get their priorities right and build families.

The abortees' orphanage is a cosmic waiting room but they are still children and they want to play. Their favourite game is dancing together in closed circles and singing back to each other to match their own collective sadness.

Because they are victims of abortion some children remain on crutches or have to wear masks to cover up the disfigurement or have patches held over socketless eyes but they still all sing together. The singing is in such low mournful tones, they feel so ashamed and don't want their parents to hear them sing so sadly but they must sing to be noticed by their protectors and guardian angels. They are also mistaken in believing as most children do that they are somehow to blame for their parents' absence and wrongdoing.

Cosmic law is such that they must be seen in dreams by loved ones and not be heard like all good children should. If parents could hear them they would hear bells and whistles in extremely low pitches beyond the human ear's ability to ascertain but certain animals such as dogs, owls and bats flying at night hear them all the time. They are tuned to such distressing signals that emit from these orphanages.

Bats whirl around in circles at the pitiful sound the children make. Mesmerized by the rhythmic hum of the synthesized voices calling back from the grave and a sound which now haunts the spheres. The bats may crash against your window at night if you live in the country, trying to wake parents up to listen to their children getting ready to leave this Planet. A bat lives in dark places and recesses like caves and such a dwelling is no fit place for a child to be out late at night looking for parental love, where normally demons are thought to hide. Where else can phantom children go for comfort and parenting? However, for some mysterious reason they are heard by birds of the night and protected from above. The birds roam the night sky searching for a baby's loved ones to shake them awake in order that they can hear their aborted children's mournful song; such loved ones as these are still stone deaf to such mournful sounds.

Protection comes not only from winged creatures of the night but also from dogs, family pets who are mysterious beings too. Consider this when your dog next tilts his ear at some unheard sound and whines for a moment listening to the aborted children's choir, hundreds of thousands of voices as they wait to move off from planet earth.

STARDUST

God's waiting room is indeed full. Owls hoot and toot and the young ones get spooked when they hear the low notes of the poor banished Eve children as they are known to the Owls. The singing is intense, equivalent to that sound created by Hildegard von Bingen, the famed 12th century Benedictine nun who wrote such extraordinary church music of celestial and heavenly quality. The music of the abortees is even more mysterious; it is like God's slow March of Progress coupled with his revolutionary thought all mixed together by baby sound to form a cosmic cement that will fasten tight His vast laws and principles to each new Planetary Cosmos like a huge footprint momentarily striding past and touching each new galaxy with His grace and love. The children sing because they have no choice; they must fill their lungs with angel song and the sound will give uplift to their broken bodies, hitching them a lift on the interstellar wind-jammer for their destination is the far-off stars past Jupiter and Mars. They are following along in God's footsteps to be made part of new families in far-off space. Unwanted here they will be loved there.

Not quite day and not quite night, these children have one foot here and one foot there. Until they leave they will have a foot in both camps, one foot for mum, the other for dad. But the aborted children, some of them terribly disfigured, don't mean any harm; they know from the angels they were not wanted but they still love their parents anyway and would run through brick walls for them and so don't hold any grudges; they are only in mourning for the family that never was. The bonds of family are so strong even great distances will not keep them apart. Even after they leave on the wind-jammer express they all one day hope to come back, to pass through a wormhole in space and gaze on their mother's face.

The children's singing is after all for their parents, real world music from every far flung corner. Vedic hymns from India, Gregorian chants from Europe, Prayers of all types and kinds from the Americas, Cymbals and Drums from Africa, Incantations from Russia and Asia. Crashing and banging, overwhelming sound from out of the mouths of babes who are ready to leave this earth forever and never to return. Like the Great Irish Hunger of the 19th century leaking Coffin ships departing home shores and their passengers knowing as they sang, 'Fare Thee Well My One True Love to the Land I Once Adored'. They knew they would never see their families, friends and homeland again.

The singing will go on and on, up to and beyond the moment of departure and on and on across the Universe. Only the sound gets louder as the distance gets longer. The pitch is so deafening and unbearable like a Banshee's Wail; they know, finally, when the children reach ten million miles from Earth, and from their parents, they will never see again except in dreams and visions. The sadness is overwhelming but after a time when the bells and whistles and voices

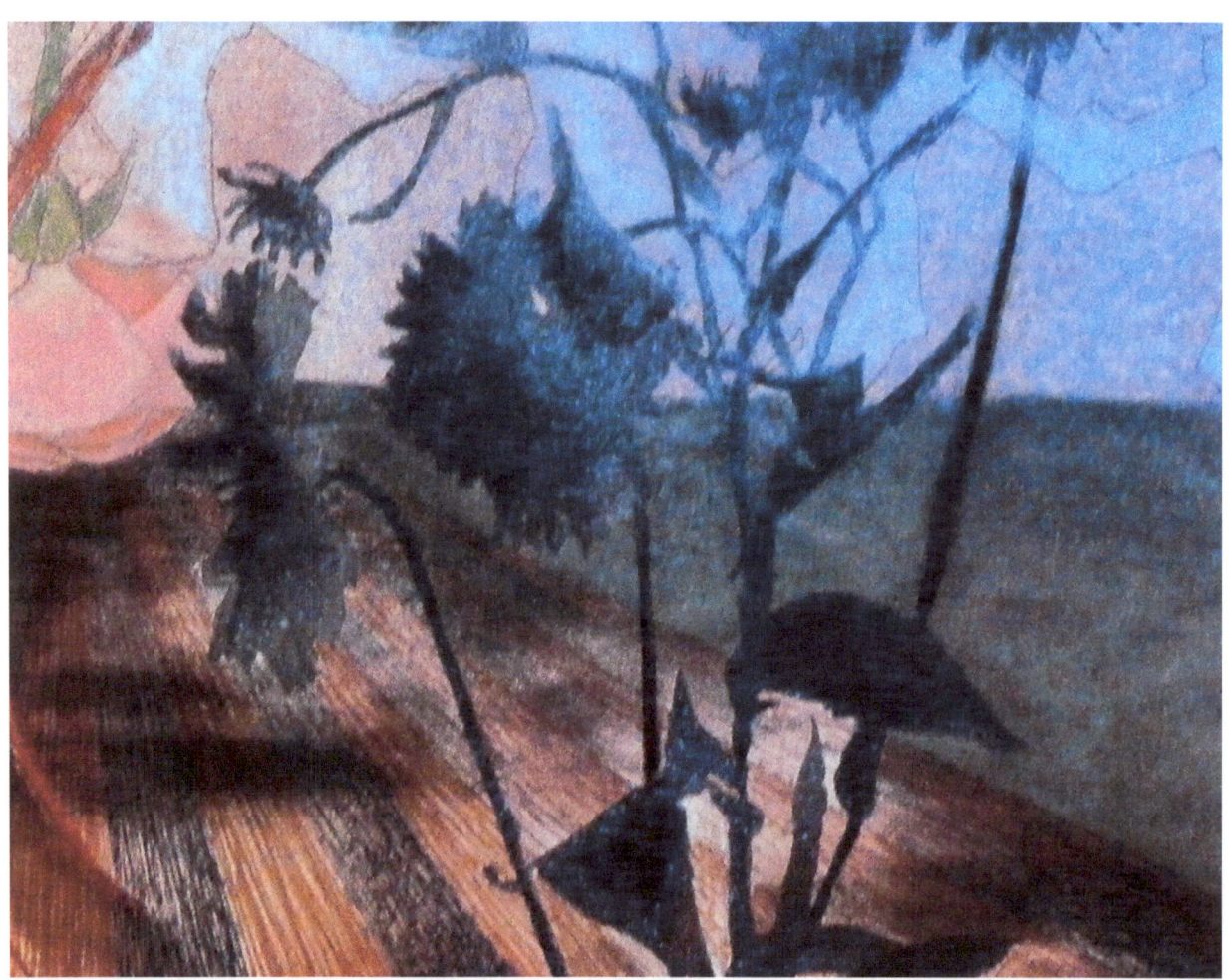

have died down the sound now has an irresistible allure and angels almost lose their minds when the children pass by on the galaxy express in an irresistibly long chain of children stretching ten thousand miles into space, holding hands and carrying bells and whistles, dancing along on the super cosmic highway.

Pity the poor parents now at home when their time comes to love again for their aborted children's voices will make up the soundtrack as they move across space. Parents of aborted children, while sleeping, will be transported to planetary parenting classes where they will have lessons on how to love a child through the many sacrifices it takes to become a real parent.

They will walk the suffering road and learn how to find the courage to raise a child, and have the brains to provide for a child and find a loving heart for a child. After all is said and done they will travel back to Earth and wake up wondering where they've been and will only faintly recall the sound of children's voices and bells and whistles formed from their unwanted children's song of Interstellar farewell.

The world still prays that one day after these parenting classes are over with, that angels will visit homesteads once again and bless former terminators for a second time with a child. And this time it will be only congratulations which are heard in the household rather than commiserations like before and that parents will have been forgiven by God and so given a second chance to love and make amends to all the aborted babies and their guardian angels by loving and raising another child. Amen ■

CLOUD CHILDREN

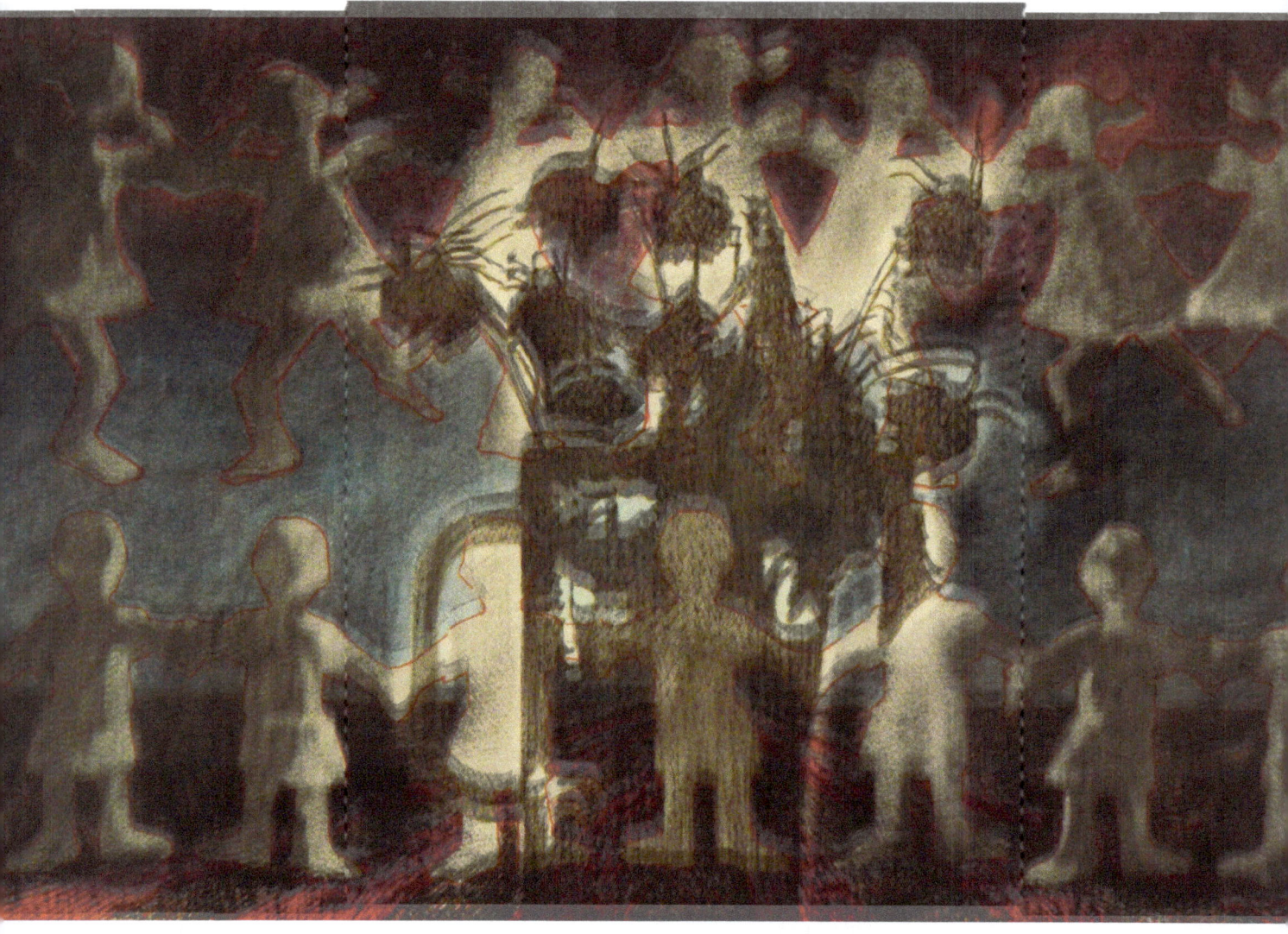

The ghost children dance through the night, not only to mourn their own passing but to highlight the excessive termination of new life. They are International Children and they worship One God the Great Spirit and also esteem their mother and father as Confucius said they should.

Below them in the painting is the dying flower cauldron of the womb still emitting jets of light like lightning rods that illuminates the children's plight and the stark nakedness of the unborn. They begin to chant: "Into this world we have come and out of this world we will go, sooner than we hoped. Our time has now come and we are together so we ask you our friends, 'will you abide

CLOUD CHILDREN

with us through the forty nights of the Unborn's Wake?'."

The aborted child's identity changes the moment after termination as they instantly become Night Travellers and Skywalkers. The children eventually depart this world but not before forty nights of active mourning are over using the Heavenly inspired Rituals of Song and Dance. The children must mourn their own passing, as parents are still too ashamed or maybe relieved so soon after termination to notice their loss.

Immediately after the medical procedure is performed the aborted babies enter a trance like state and travel back headlong down a new spiral birth canal. They go through a tunnel at breakneck speed and then suddenly they stop and behold their fellow babies' previous Incarnations and all accompanied with colours of emerald lights having all the power of a thousand suns. Within this moment the gift of second sight is given to them, then a big bang is heard carrying them through into a new dimension and this is followed by immense silence, while before them is knowledge of hundreds of thousands of their former life-times. The experience is similar to noticing for the first time a mountain vista suddenly appearing through the clouds. They now understand they have once been every form of existence known and unknown, good and bad, happy and sad, rich and poor, tired, sick and old, youthful, beautiful and married, father and mother, brother and sister to every kind of being. Moving forward with every root and branch, every leaf of moss, to form that oneness of communion, merging every crystal fibre of their being with their Maker. They have been every cotton bud, every animal in the kingdom, every insect tiny world, every kind of relative to friend and foe alike. Your King and Queen, beggar man thief, male and female, butcher, baker, candlestick maker. These insights are the two gifts of Seeing bestowed on the aborted foetus as a result of enforced termination. This gift from the angels demonstrates the continuum of all existence and is meant as a soothing balm. It does not lessen the pain nonetheless of separation from their mother for the children.

From the time we crawled out of the sea and evolved, information has been kept and decoded in our DNA like some time capsule held in an Arctic Ice cap. Starting from fluid bacteria of non-visible life form, to single cell Amoeba, through to various mutations of life evolving from amphibians, invertebrate, vertebrates, reptiles and birds and then we leap to mammals. Having been touched by the Lord and showered with His gifts of second sight, unborn baby law has understood all that has gone before them from the cradle of evolution to the unfolding of His love that reaches and pinnacles in a child's heart. What is not written is our response to a baby's heart. That is something still unknown and only to be told through our own hands and actions.

The baby journey of visiting past lives quickly moves on like a ticking bomb to the dawn of Homo Sapiens in Africa, fast forward out of Africa to Europe and North America and we see many shadows cast from the cave fire. Dwellings populated by family groups and tribes with still half wild dogs kept as working pets crawling close to the fire mesmerized by the source of heat and warmth. Flickering through the flames like moving pictures are the cave drawings of primitive man showing his creative genius, his impressions of the natural world: Hunters, Antelope, Mammoth, wild Deer, long horn Cattle, Buffalo, Elk, Tiger, Lions and packs of running, hungry Wolves. The children stop and watch awhile the shadows on the wall. They hum, 'All that has been and will be will come to pass.'

What has made them who they are as beings worthy of respect is Spirit Law. Manifested through the ages by Evolution and God's love. Their demise as children has come because of instant gratification by someone who maybe called too soon or arrived too late. But that was of yesterday, and before too long their mind's eye begins to wander because there are new wonders to behold. They must return to the dance; it has begun again.

There is a sudden rustle and movement as a quiver goes through the multitude of aborted souls. Suddenly the great Tee-Pee Dance is underway, the very font of worship is here on show. All around them is cascading, sparkling light; they swing like moths to a flame. Flying and flinging themselves like a Highland Caber, they whoop and shout their song unheard into the night. In this way they communicate with the stars of the night sky, the compass points of star ships. They are building up their strength through song for their journey to the outermost cosmos to inhabit the new star systems now being born. They are the new stardust or baby mist of planetary life.

A children's lullaby is on their sweet baby lips and it is sung for the constant new arrivals. Round and round they go, never stopping, only going faster and faster into a whirl of dervish mist until they disappear into a cipher and only to reappear the next night. This continues for forty nights mirroring Christ's fast, his mysterious time spent alone in the desert battling with the devil's seductive dreams. Where the children go during the day is a mystery of the dance and of the guardian angels. Some say they take their daytime rest in Christ's tomb in Jerusalem, and like him when their time is come they will ascend into heaven before a quire of angels and assembled Star Ships.

The children who dance never touch the earth; they are ethereal. They belong now to the spirit realm, that vast mysterious space between us and the next world. Their life journey was sadly interrupted by their termination. Lessons meant to be learned here will have to be taken elsewhere. The Universe records it all – nothing is missed in God's great ledger.

The last frontier of the Human experience is of the spirit realm, the inner exploration of the soul. We have measured the distance between the stars and developed microscopes to fathom the tiniest speck of dust. We still remain ignorant of ourselves and our passions and are still subject to them unless and without calling on God's help we are lost. As lost as unborn children are to this world.

46
CLOUD CHILDREN

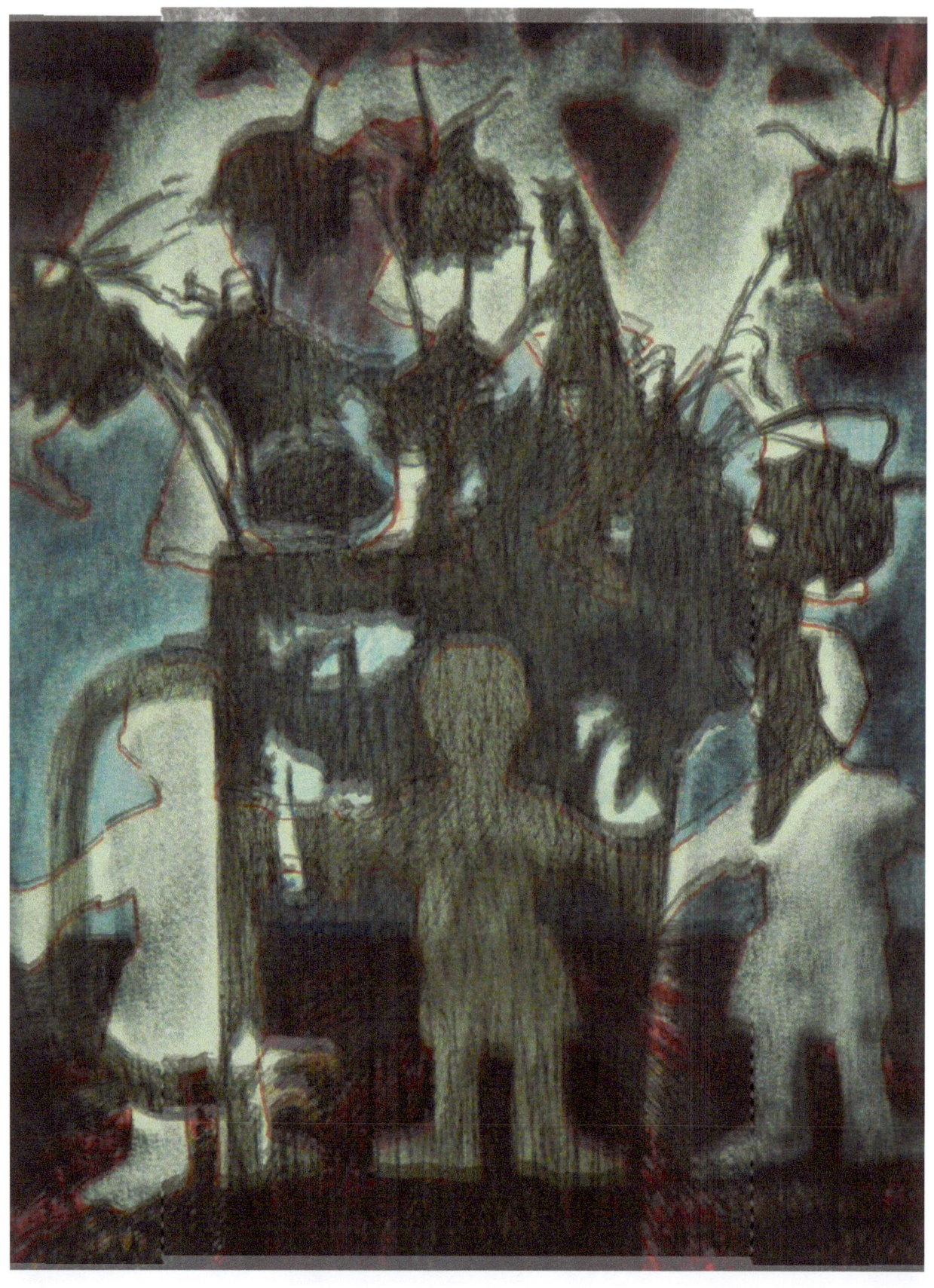

CLOUD CHILDREN

After forty nights the swaddling children are now officially Lords of the Dance. They suddenly stop dancing and enter into silence and begin to march over the horizon and swim like swordfish through seven seas and walk twice around the moon and back again. The Owl and the Pussy Cat wave them goodbye. Humpty Dumpty who had a great fall is sponsoring the unborn children into nursery rhyme law and is their self appointed spokesperson. He leads the silent dancers, strutting his stuff out front like a majorette but is always ready to offer soothing support to the aborted children and explain to them the concept of Broken Glass. Jack and Jill from Up over the Hill carry their Pail of Water to slake the children's thirst.

All the King's Horses and all the King's Men who could not put Humpty Dumpty back together again have come along to take their leave of the departing nearly children. They know all the sweet, tiny kidlets are leaving this protected fantasy world of little people. They will always be babies to all the king's horses and all the king's men, forever in the memory of the Earth and therefore always be part of this Alice in Wonderland, down the Rabbit hole world, created for them as children. They will always be cherished and made part of fairy law and will hear again tall tales told of the magic vine of Jack and the Beanstalk, of the Giant's barrelling crescendo voice, "fee, fie, fo, fum" and the story of the three bears and their missing breakfast porridge or of the Little Mermaid of Denmark and all the rest of the characters who live in the world of Children's imagination and fairy tales.

Good King Wenceslas of frosty mornings is there with the children. He is lying underneath the fiery flames warming his old bones, tickling his beard and taking his deep rest. In fact all of the characters found in Children's Nursery Rhymes have appeared on this evening scene of "All Souls" bringing the love of childhood to the fore on this tumultuous night of sorrows and demonstrating their support for the departing Skywalkers who they will never get to cherish in real time through their wonderful tales of thrilling childhood imagination.

However there are some sinister twists on old favourite stories told by Hans Christian Andersen and the Brothers Grimm. These are special new edition books, much darker tales than the originals and kept secret until now. Tales of Hansel and Gretel and Little Red Riding Hood which were especially composed for nobody's child. The wily children of the 3rd eye eagerly pick up these new books of folk tales that truly represent their short twenty first century life on earth.

Children's toys now take shape and form up behind each other and storm across the sky, raising an angry dust before the children's final departure call. Tin soldiers from every toy shop across the land have woken up and now March for Life up and down the sky in a new protest song, "We want Life, we want Life". To the tune of left right left right. Retired Majors in seaside homes hold pow-wows. Gold braided Brigadiers holding ceremonial swords who, drinking spearmint freshly mashed tea with their friends, the retired Generals, want to take up command once again of their mobilized toy land troops and demand protection for unborn children from their talking shop Politicians and Prime Ministers, the Mr Gladstones and Disraelis of this world who make up the rules for Toy Town's law and order.

The Toy Sergeant Major barks out orders from the parade ground, "Rapunzel, let down your hair" and she obeys and lets down her hair and the children's toys scramble from her crown and pour down her long locks like refugees to meet the abortees. Together they go out to meet their navigators, Prince Charming and Cinderella, who greet them all two by two, one boy and one girl and love them and settle them down for the Space flight. The Stewards come along next and feed them with ready made children's meals of Captain Birdseye fish fingers or pizza, chips and beans followed by chocolate cake, sweets and treacle tart. Afterwards singing mermaids floating on pieces of coral come along the aisles, washing and dressing the children in blue and pink spot pyjamas, getting them ready for bed.

CLOUD CHILDREN

After all the excitement of forty nights of singing and dancing the Wake is finally over and the babies will soon be gone from this world. Meanwhile in the cockpit the sky pilots are ready to take the evacuated children to their new home beyond the stars, securing them a peaceful life far away from bogus incubators, incinerators, terminators and anything else that harms a child in this world of cruelty and no love we have made for the unborn. The starship flight crew stand and say a prayer moments before departure as engines are firing up all around and systems are ready to go into full steam ahead. The abortees' prayer goes like this:

Oh Dear Lord, please hear us, with the gentle crest of your hand and with the lasting touch of sweetness of your bloodied, wounded Palm please rock the cradle tonight and give us undisturbed rest. We badly need your caressing love, Dear Lord, in order to fall asleep and rest in your peace and grace. For after all, Lord, what we have seen and been through in our short lives we need all your love now more than ever, Dear Father. Please hear us.

After the prayer is said all the babies, all 211,000 strong, who have already been fed, washed and put to bed by mermaids have now fallen fast asleep with their toys and nursery rhymes beside them. ■

PALMS OF OUR LORD

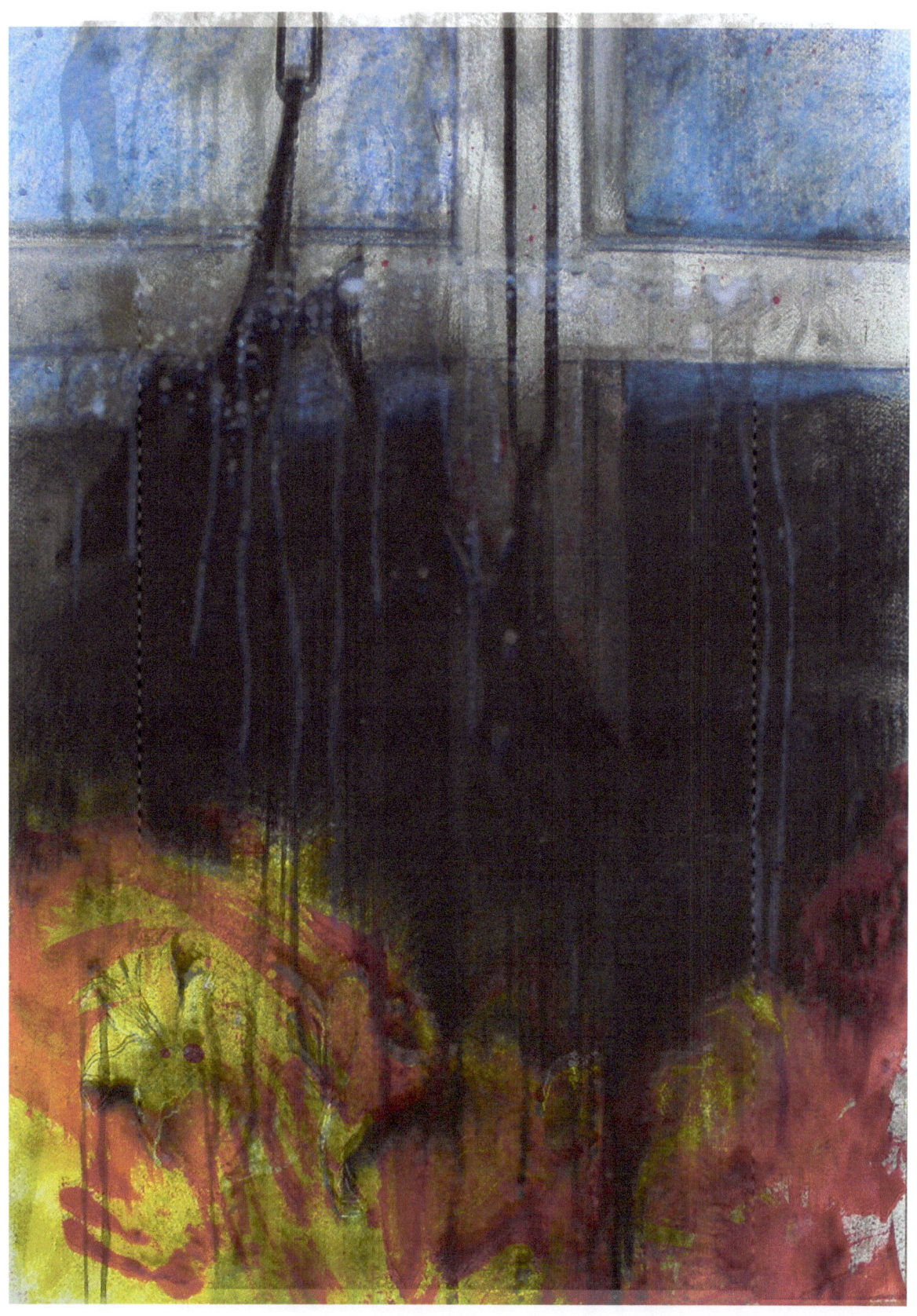

PALMS OF OUR LORD

The face of the baby is in the ruins of the abortion. It can be read like a Palm reader reads a hand. It is also written in the stars by our Lord's hand. Clear strokes of magical calligraphy, written with the Master's quill. Heart and lungs came first and impregnated with traces of gold and copper. The brain is formed next; the mind we share with God, and with it are traces of silver and minerals of old. The ideas we think are there long before we ourselves even begin to believe them. Only our own evolution as social beings and our own true brotherhood awaits these thoughts unfolding. Though thoughts eventually do come bidden and framed from the Colour House where thoughts are made. Like a chocolate factory of space they turn out ideas of nature's law and order wrapped and ready to be opened. Prophets of gold and silver are present when the heart and head are working in sync. Silver is the colour of clearness of thought; all things emanate from this reservoir of colour. Dreaming ideas await to be transformed through wisdom and then unlocked through reason and logic and then made ready to be understood by our own effort and application. Only then will they pass out on the parade ground of discovery, and every Nobel laureate worth his salt knows all about these press ups of thought and this continuous weight lifting of the mind. It will always pay out in dividends time and again.

What is it that God wants us to think? Only to be our own true selves of whom we really are born to be and that is married to His principle of laws. Remember all is sacred mystery; each rock and leafy tree has its own destiny of dreams. All is becoming in the celestial chest of drawers of thought. That's why the stars shine so brightly; they are simply thoughts that stream their speed of dreaming on to each new baby being. All babies are real receivers of God's all loving and creative thoughts.

The divine connection of dreaming comes from their own inherent starlight dust. It keeps shining in them until that time the stardust finally turns to ashes and life is scattered to the winds of the four quarters and comes to rest upon the waters of the seven oceans deep. Now oozing and birthing again in the celestial

52
PALMS OF OUR LORD

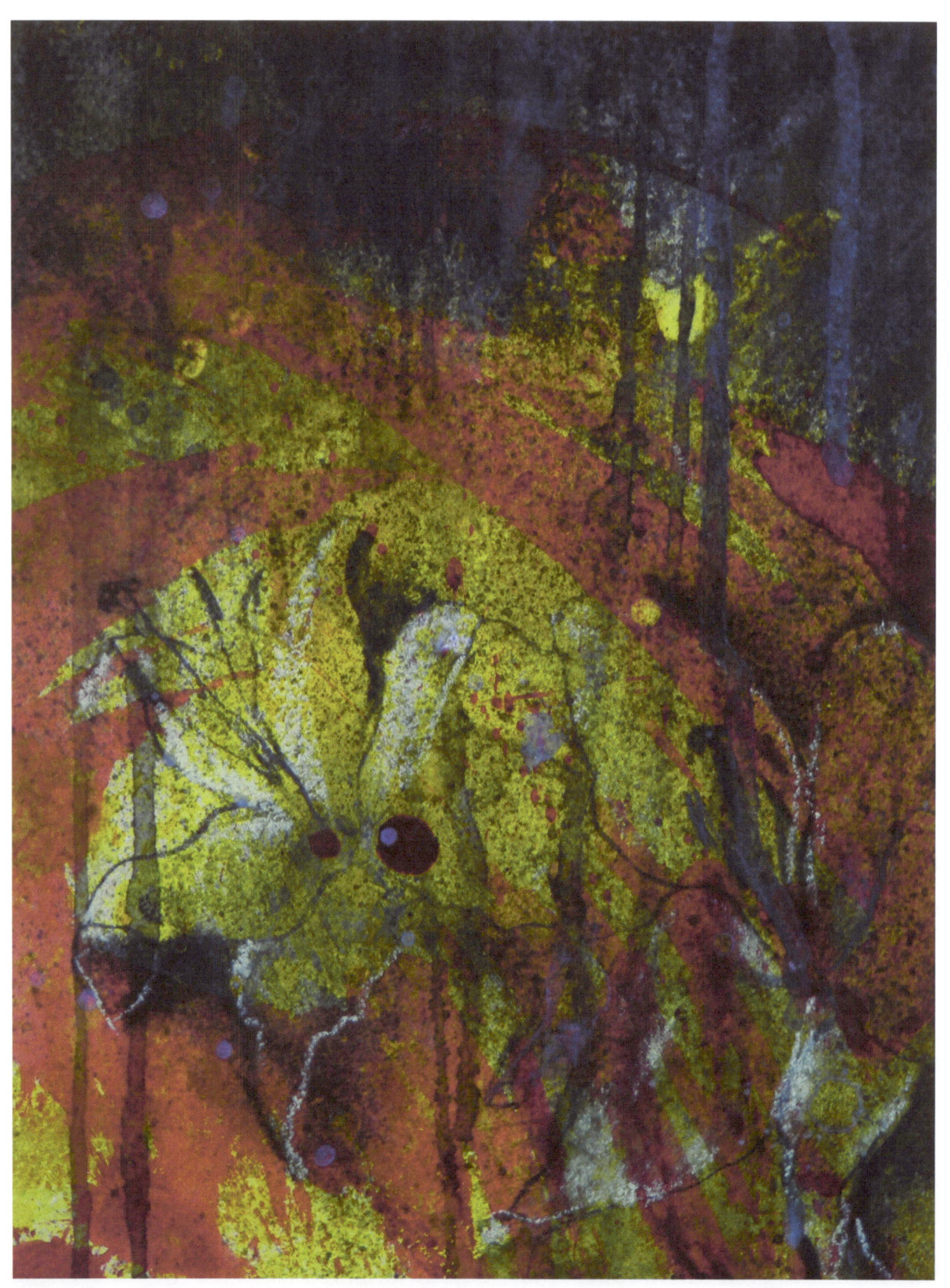

soup it becomes more star dust to dust. Babies are stars of light and dreaming and breathed into life by God's Holy Spirit.

What mystery lies in the unformed mind of a baby? What sacred mystery of life comes from the stars and is held in the palm of God and will only be truly appreciated through the prism of our Lord's wounded hands and feet and His pierced side and out again into the infinity of our space-bound future?

The children are stars of stars and they first reach out their hand towards the stars, their true destination and home. Their future is to be with all the other stars of Father Time, one day becoming a supernova of stars which light up the universe in pulses of gold and silver in a rainbow of colour and a cacophony of sound. Hark the Herald! The angels are singing.

Palm Sunday our Lord rode through Jerusalem on a donkey; the people came out to greet him with date palms lain at his feet. He blessed the air they breathed and purified their thoughts by his message of love and deliverance. The apostles were the first to see the hands of the Lord where the nails had pierced the flesh. To look through our Lord is to see infinity; our destination and point of departure is the dreaming. To look down we see only suffering, the rising damp of shadow; it eclipses the blue sky that symbolises our glory. Shadow comes and the old shaman is present and is in tune with both worlds, the world of form and the spirit world. He looks through entrails of Gore and sees the past, present and future. As the damp rises and the little spirit of a baby hovers over the sinking body of Gore he comes to its aid and stands there being a breath of love, now breathing in the spirit of the baby through petalled nosebleeds and transports its life force of love to the Chariot of Angels. Guardian angels who wait patiently with unicorns ready to fly off to the stars. Poor parents of yore, your baby child will wait to love you still, for it is written in the stars, when your turn comes to be carried off to the heavens you will love again. Your passion itself fired up the furnace of love and nature will not be denied its innocence.

54
PALMS OF OUR LORD

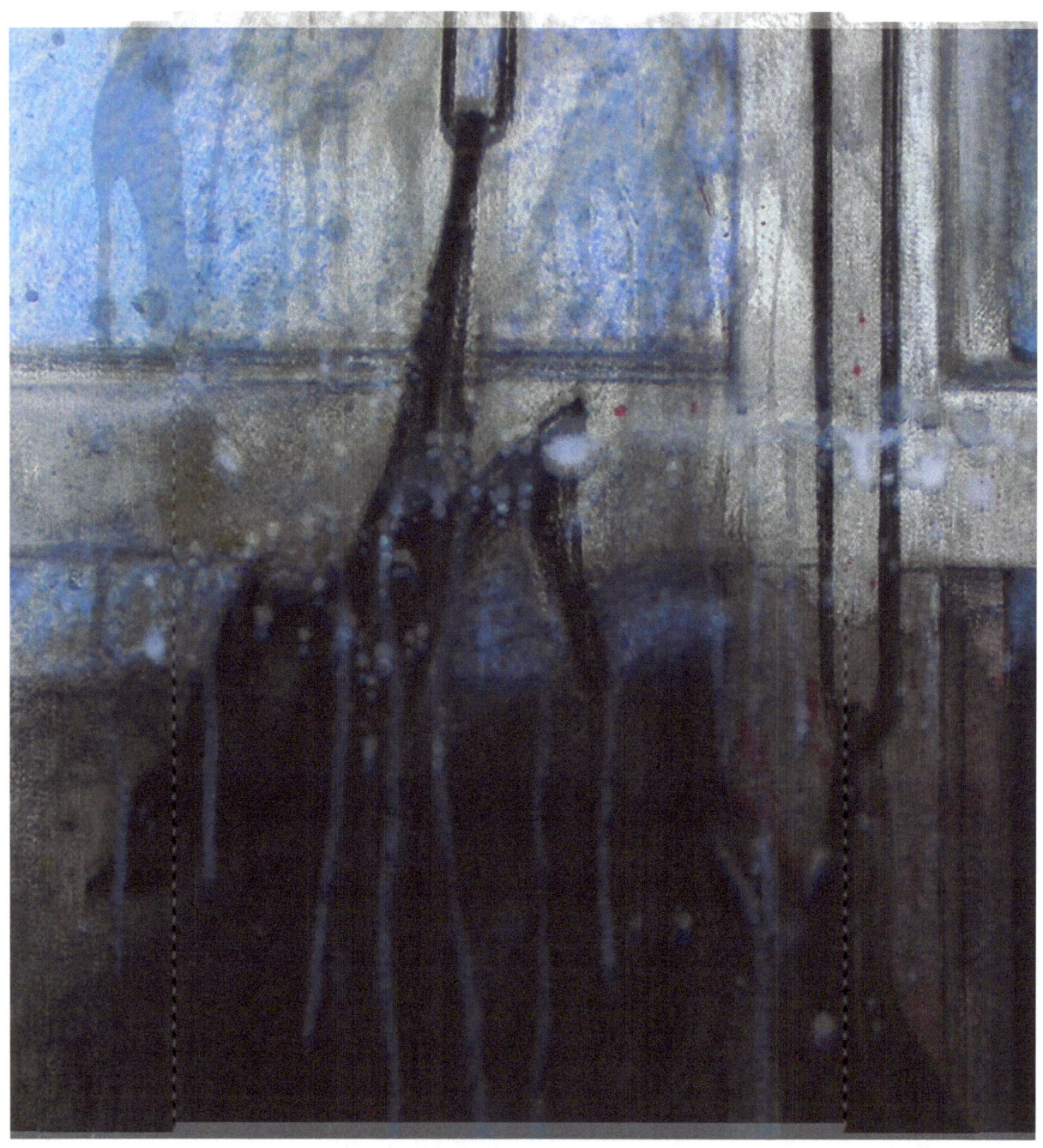

Heaven knows we freeze our heart when we shut out love and become hardened and cynical about life. Then it will take a child's love to thaw out the poor old soak we have become. The Mother dreams her dreams of guilt and shame and one day maybe soon she will wake up straight as if hit like a thunderbolt. She will hang up her shoes in sorrow and look through the window of dreams and see only darkness where a baby should have been.

PALMS OF OUR LORD

To look at the after birth of an abortion is to read the Tarot of Ruins. Petals of Lily and gold are now speckled with red. No Bumble Bee of old with striped jacket and yellow trousers of honey will transform life's nectar into a trusty Beehive of love. No school of bees will be heard buzzing in the valley of the Lily. The purity of Our Lady the Queen of Heaven will never reach out to touch such a Bumble Bee or comfort her school of lost aborted stars. Such children are not wasted, they will lighten up the blackness of outer space as the universe is expanding and needs starlight. The aborted foetus is taken back to the stars by angels riding on chariots of gold to be blessed by our Lord Jesus and bathed in the blood of the lamb. They will be one again now wrapped in the shroud of Christ as they become the very body of our Lord. So now when we, the poor children of Eve, eat of his flesh and drink of his blood; when we share at our Lord's last supper, we will also do this in memory of the unborn. He has taken them into the body of Christ. Their flesh is now his flesh; their spilt blood is his spilt blood and their own innocence is Christ's own innocence foretold. Rest now, poor little aborted babies and don't you cry. You are within the body of our little Lord Jesus and you will sit at his right hand, at the table of the feast of the last supper. And we, the poor children of Eve, are still your brothers and sisters in the body of Christ and as you become one with the Lord of hosts through the mystery of the last supper of love. We who eat this bread and drink of this cup will do this always in memory of You.

SUICIDE

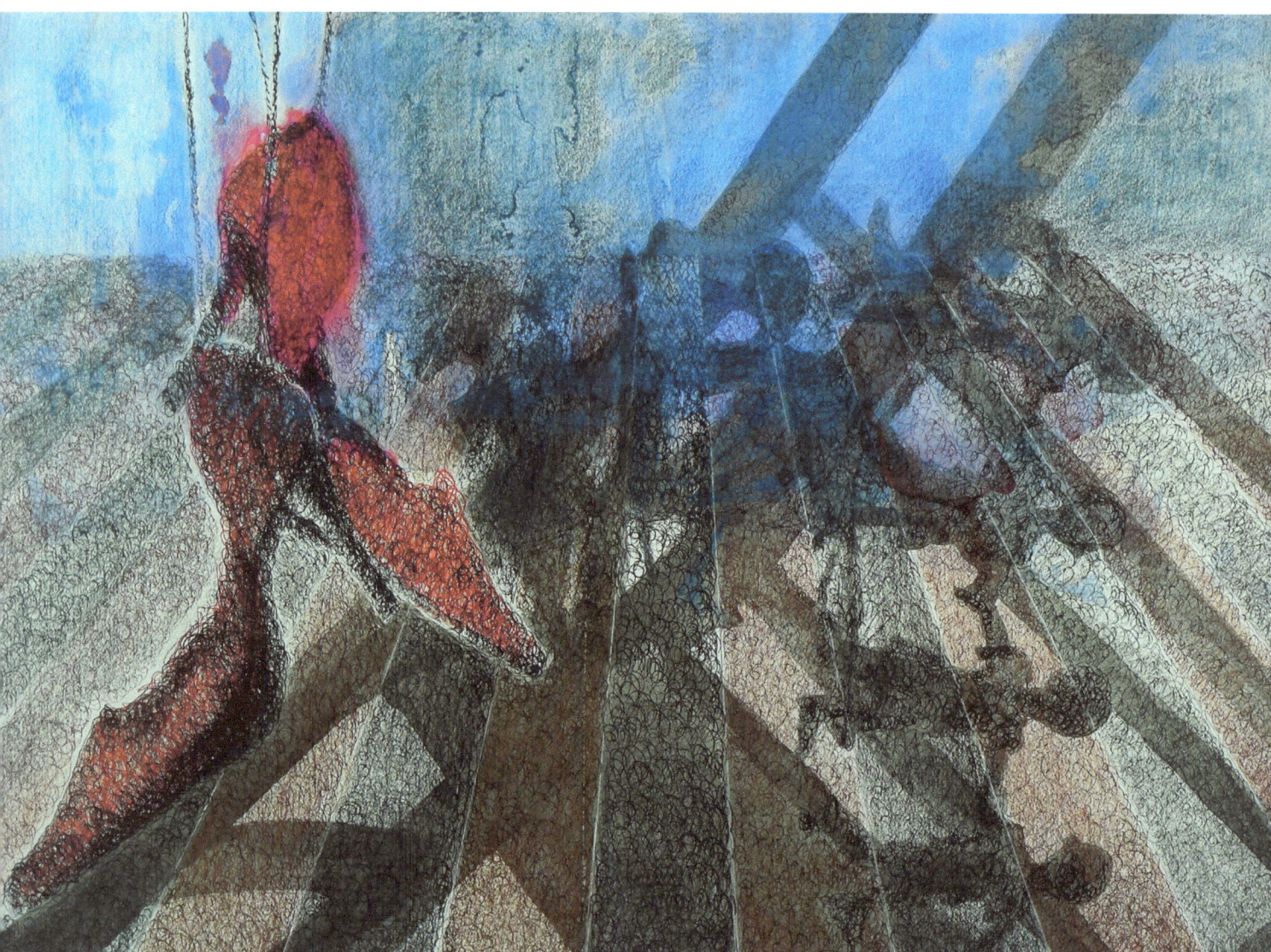

Of all the killing going on in the world today does a woman choose to slaughter her own flesh and blood? With my partner there were lots of excuses but no compelling reason to have an abortion. There wasn't a medical dilemma as she was perfectly healthy. She was in a loving relationship, she wasn't being abused or felt herself a victim. It just came down to convenience and fear of financial insecurity and being a mum for the first time. But surely being fearful for the future and pregnant is a part of any healthy woman's life? It's a natural reaction. Why should a corporation and her GP be so readily allowed to play on that fear and offer a quick fix solution and at what cost? The price is paid with the blood of an innocent life and the financial expense to the NHS, millions of pounds of public money to euthanize a baby, to say nothing of the future harm to one's Soul of such a premeditated action. It may seem at the time like a solution to some parents and that no real harm is done, like having a tooth pulled out, but give it some years and those baby fears will come back to haunt a parent. All they can reach for at the end of the day is the Prozac or the therapist couch. No breastfeeding, no cuddles of love, no hearing an infant's first words, no seeing their toddler's first gleeful steps, no first day at school, in fact no memories at all.

The abortion clinic is a jerry built commercial terminator of a parent's soul. The world has been turned upside down and is standing on its head. The clinic, presented to look corporate and caring, is an oxymoron, of course, but who cares? Not the corporation after the deed is done. Afterwards what matters is the eternal world; the hidden dimension, the truth, God and a parent's relationship to this truth which in the end is not relative at all. What is at stake here is the very stuff of life for women have the God given instinct and means of creating and caring for children. All women by nature are potential mothers and there is no denying this fact or of the real happiness and fulfilment that comes from motherhood. Walk through any park on a sunny afternoon and observe the joy on show between many young mums and their children.

A woman's status does change when she becomes pregnant as she is now two persons in one body and whether a woman is two weeks, six weeks or twenty four weeks pregnant, she is a mother to that child she is carrying and must bear some responsibility to this new life and how she came to be in that condition in the first place. The child didn't ask to be put there but is there nevertheless.

Many women for one reason or another are now pushing motherhood further and further back, some into their mid 30s and even early 40s before starting a family. Some still want to pursue only a career which is their choice. Others,

SUICIDE

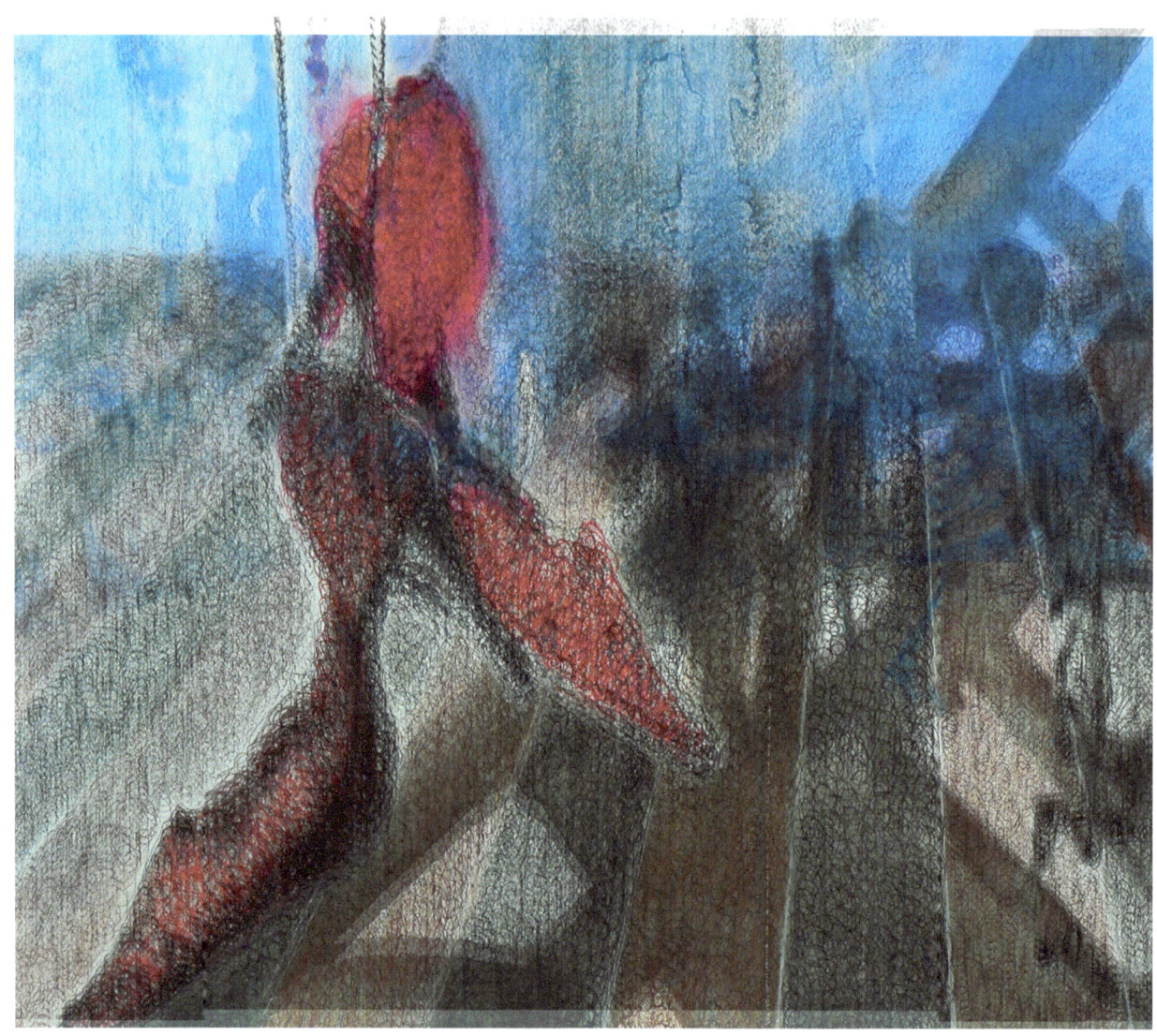

usually some of the most able and astute, lead desolate lives on the inside and have become mistaken in their core beliefs, having lost their way in life and are now nothing more than consumers and pill poppers; believing money and ego will solve all their problems: a summation of modern woman in search of a soul perhaps? The archetype of this type of woman is the daily commuter of the home counties beltway, carrying fancy handbags and wearing expensive clothes, making money for the corporate state as if this could be a substitute for motherhood. She must succeed in this man's world and be tough. She must have the edge and be a real go-getter, a bread winner. She has nerves of steel and proves it in her business dealings; she will always wear the pants at home. She

SUICIDE

has learned through appraisal after appraisal the eyes of the corporate elite are watching her so she has become highly competitive, almost aggressive, and must succeed in everything she does. On the outside she conforms to being just like a man. Don't show feelings, act as if you don't have any, carry a stiff upper lip, don't tremble and don't cry. Work becomes her life, money is her king. Status becomes everything. She is the hostess with the "mostest" and is all but married to the idea of the corporate state, making money and the devil take the hindmost.

The painting depicts the callous nature of this type of Corporate Affair and its outcome on human beings. This is a picture, indeed a caricature, of a woman who made a mistake, who got herself in trouble, who has had an abortion and afterwards committed suicide in her heart. Finally waking up to what is really important in life she finds it's far too late to change her decision even if she vows, "never again" to herself for she has been conned, like many other women before, into executing their child. In the drawing, the toppled over chair, the cut out children, are scattered all around her as the stool crashes to the floor. What we see left hanging are her red stiletto shoes, symbolic of the career she has chosen over her baby. A woman's soul is what is killed when that awful decision to abort is made, kicking over that gallows tree and leaving her heart swinging there in the wind like an old dead branch. With it goes her child, hanging there too and looking into her eyes: an intimate and gruesome death cuddle. As in life so in death. Take the money and run, career mum, but just see how far you get before your past catches up with you again. Your aborted baby, now misshapen like a Texas chainsaw massacre victim, will pursue you down the years like the Hound of heaven in your dreams and even fill your waking moments as you face the future childless and alone. ▪

NIGHT FLOWERS

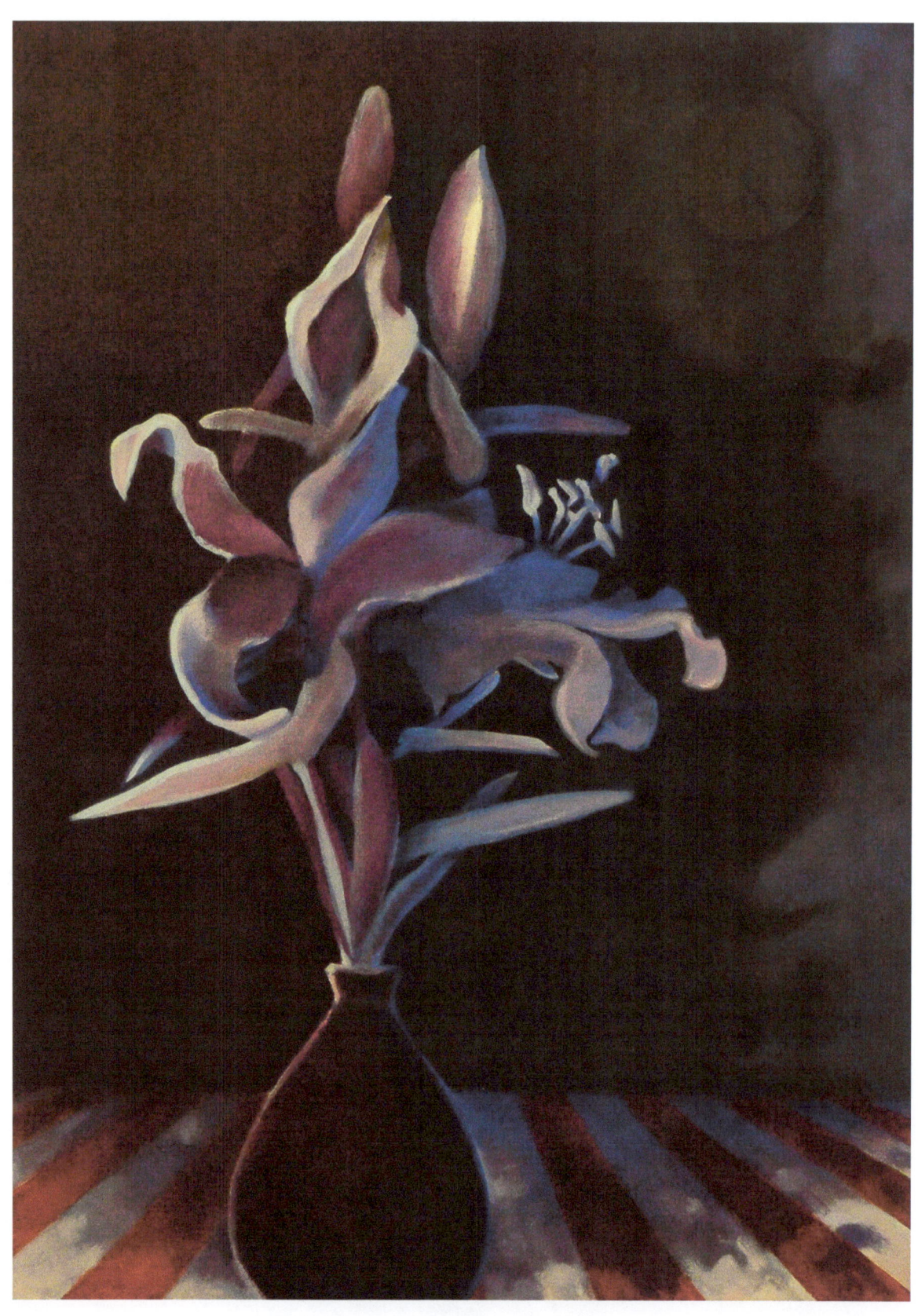

NIGHT FLOWERS

The night flowers are post apocalyptic plants; their day has now become night. They resemble a hollow victory and point towards the aftermath of a nuclear war. They have a bunker mad mentality that has come off its hinges. This self centred mentality has made life above ground impossible and when even nature is forced to live below ground by blasts of radiated heat: we have a problem.

From now on and for a long time to come we will live in secret, away from the dead heat above ground, like characters in a HG Wells novel, a time machine trip into our star spangled future, ruled over by secrets of our past and demons of the future.

Abortion has now morphed into euthanasia law, the two terrible twins. The law of demons holds sway over who will live and who can die often by drone. The night flower, like a resurrected rose in Harlem, is God's witness to what has become of His creation. When even God is forced underground humanity is at crisis point.

Babies are no longer born to women in the old fashioned way, as deformities are so commonplace and the womb is now considered a dead zone. Science has perfected its reproductive art. Babies are inseminated in a test tube and some will live and others will be farmed; their bodies are kept alive only to grow organs for transplants.

The houses are full of smoke. Abortion law has become an abortion war against the unborn. If the violence begins in the womb what chance is there it will stay there? The answers are already known and lie buried within us through the Cosmic law of transformation. By breathing in the smoke of hate we breathe out the smoke of love. In this way we smoke out the badness planted all around us from the dead zone above ground. Like some Martian landscape whose soil must be fertilized with nutrients to produce oxygen and food to sustain life. So

NIGHT FLOWERS

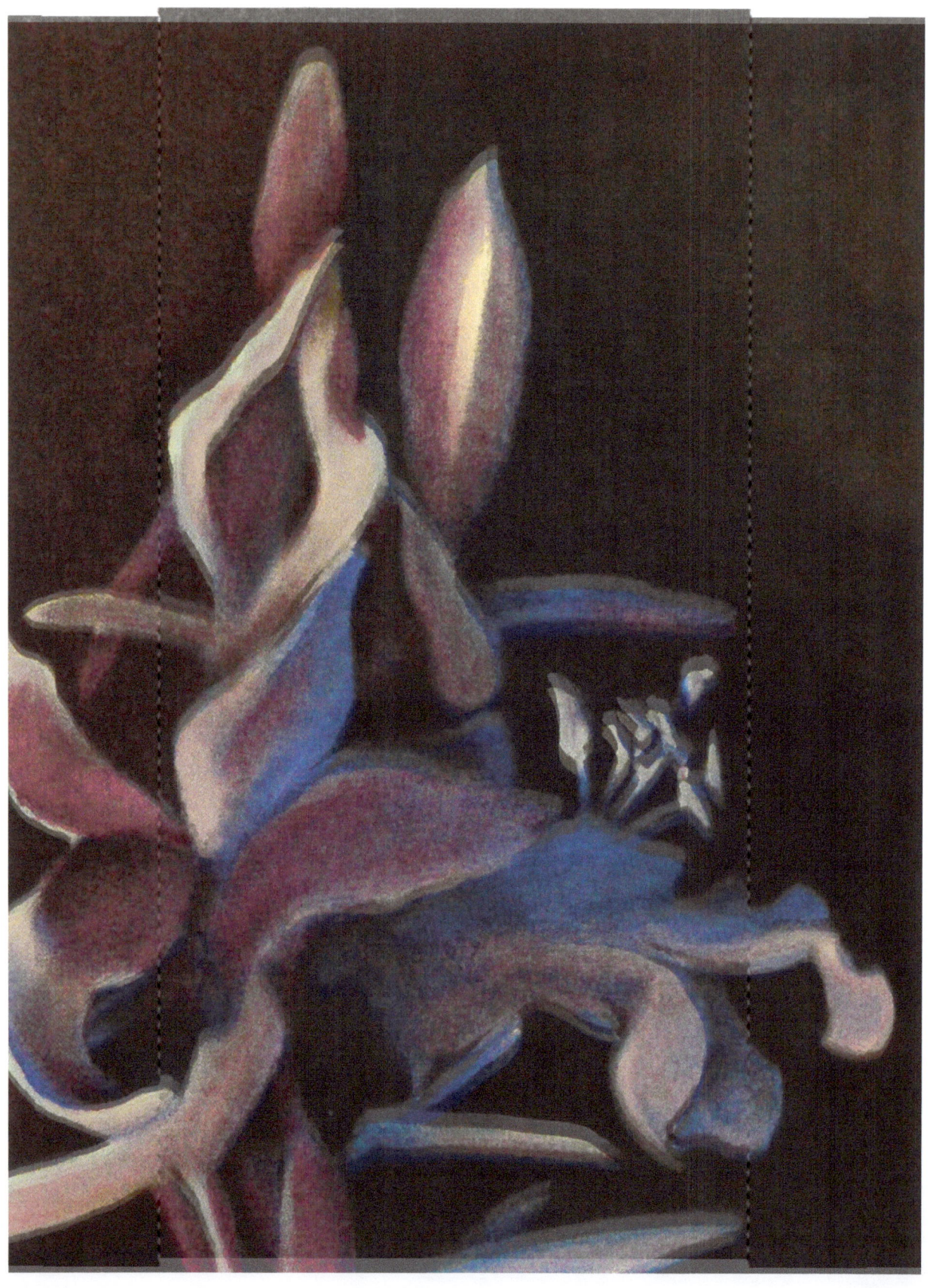

NIGHT FLOWERS

our love must regenerate our own barren earthen landscape with every breath we take, breathing love in and breathing love out. We dream when Night flowers will live in sunlight once more and where God will reign for ever in our hearts through love shown for one and other.

SUNFLOWERS

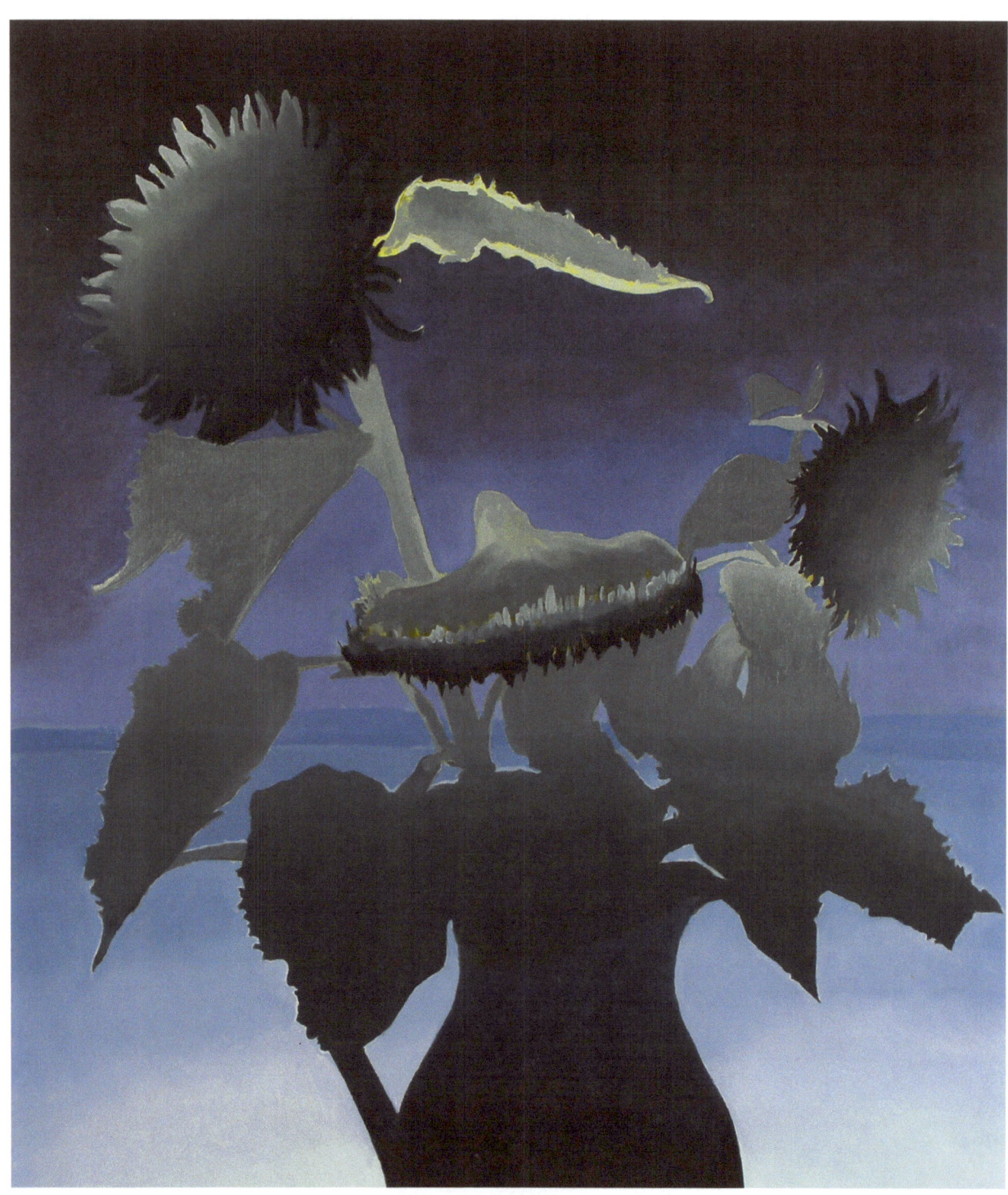

In the current dark era of Orwellian doublespeak the Kali Yuga is upon us, as foretold, the age of quarrel and destruction is here, the four horsemen of the apocalypse are running amok upon an open Pandora's box of chaos. Among the tumult there is a silent sunflower world being destroyed, on an industrial scale, stripped of all colour, identity and humanity. It has no parent or guardian worthy of the name and the new world order will not give it a second chance to live. The sunflower, in contrast to chaos, has overwhelming silent dignity; its branches made for love hang limp like a rain soaked emotion of longing. Here in this sunflower world lives the unborn. Hidden from view their short lives are cast in perpetual shadow, their one reality is their mother's womb; this place of sanctuary has been made a death row chamber: a twenty four week ticking Tot.

The unborn and unwanted have failed to reach their full nine month gestation, their heavenly due date, because their status as an aborted foetus is just an unregistered non person, a legal black hole; a non-being without rights or favour, a philosopher's conundrum, a National Health statistic.

Looking closely at the sunflower in shadowlands it seeks to live. It has the circuit board of life, electricity; these currents of love are pulses of life and they remain within the flower unto death.

At the point of termination, the illusion of life remains within the foetus. It may seem like a sick parody, a reflex action of nature or put simply a chicken run, as you will observe the same of animals the moment after decapitation and viewed on each slaughter day down on the local factory farm. A beheaded chicken will run, for a few moments, in a headless fashion before collapsing in a jerking heap.

Meanwhile at the Abu Ghraib maximum security prison where dead men are walking the last mile of life and their fate is sealed, even they still hold out a glimmer of hope, for a stay of execution, some governor's pardon. They have much more of a chance of escaping the noose or the chair through due process that the picture of innocence now being dragged out from the womb each day of the year.

66
SUNFLOWERS

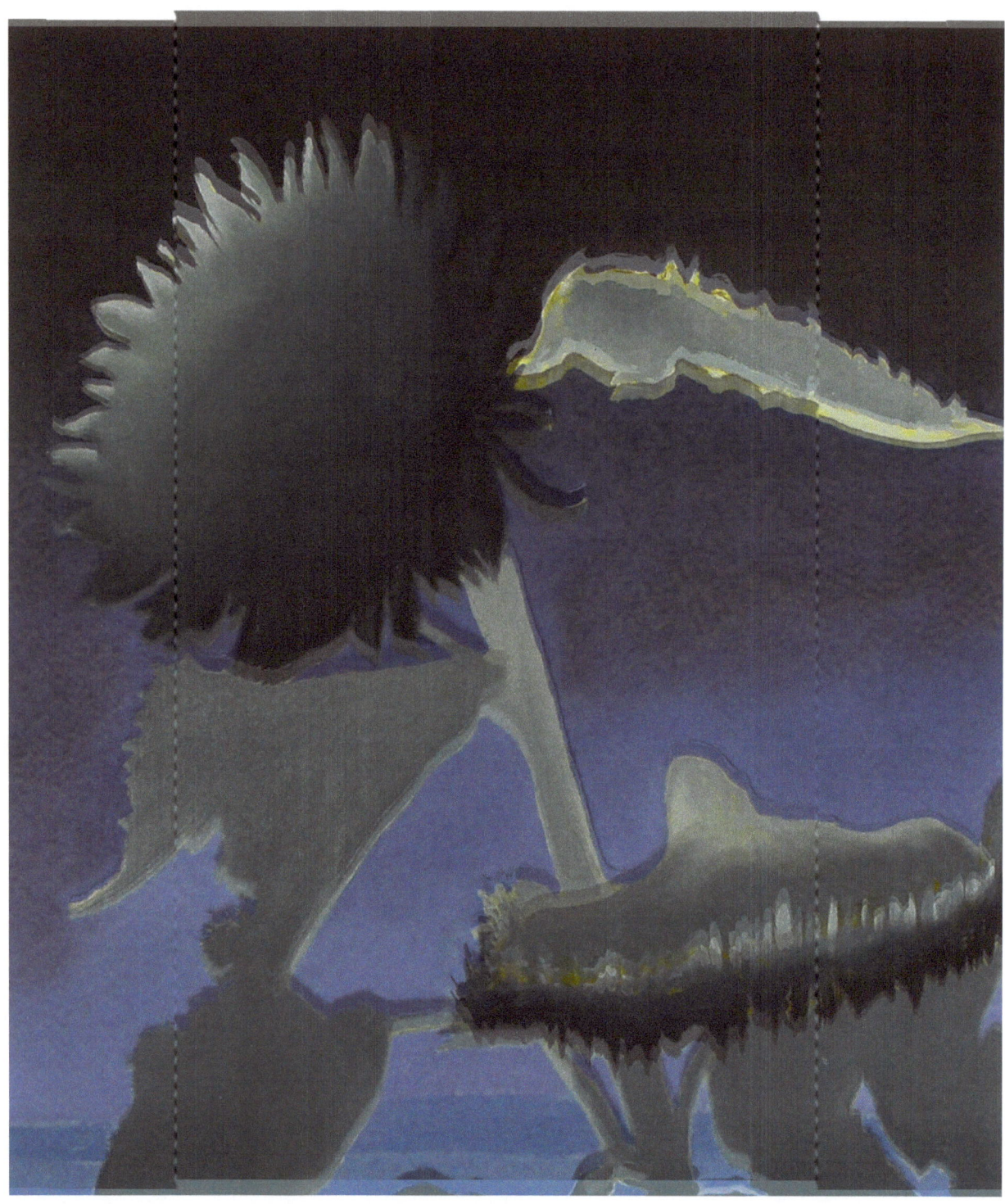

The foetus struggles to survive within its own yoke. The Stem rebel won't give up on life and even though the battle is lost and shadowlands are beckoning, the war of the Flowers will go on. It will continue onward until the sacrifice of

SUNFLOWERS

sack after sack of scrambled yoke is shown mercy and allowed to live. Because no chicken law will ever stand in the way of God's love.

Look at the sun flower, the symbol of the Sun: It strives desperately to reach out upwards towards life and where the sun should be and like a child's dashed hopes or a young girl's unrequited love. The baby shower day of joy will never come for these tots. The condemned foetus will never live to see their mummy or daddy, much less be their pride and joy.

In the sinister refugee world we have created, only moon flowers and moonlight stare back. In contrast to the stubborn little flower stretching out for the sun, the other two Moon Flower Stems are cowed like Josef Mengele twins and have quickly entered their somer holiday. The triumvirate law has created a world of perpetual moonlight, a world without reproduction where life is ruled out before it has even barely begun.

The abortion clinic is the first of the somer holiday camps: a babies' graveyard. The parentless moon-flowers on their lonely planet standing sentinel for centuries like Easter island statues, stay there, mysterious, looking out across far horizons; they will one day give Nuremberg witness to their own bloody story.

What will the condemned baby experience before the hammer blow of abortion happens? It will witness an unknown foe dressed in a doctor's apron and a surgical mask. The child will feel only that last stab of pain as the sun flower light goes out and becomes perpetual moonlight grey. It is done, the boulder of innocence has been scraped. The empty womb. The bird has flown. Lark ascending.

BREAKFAST FOR ONE

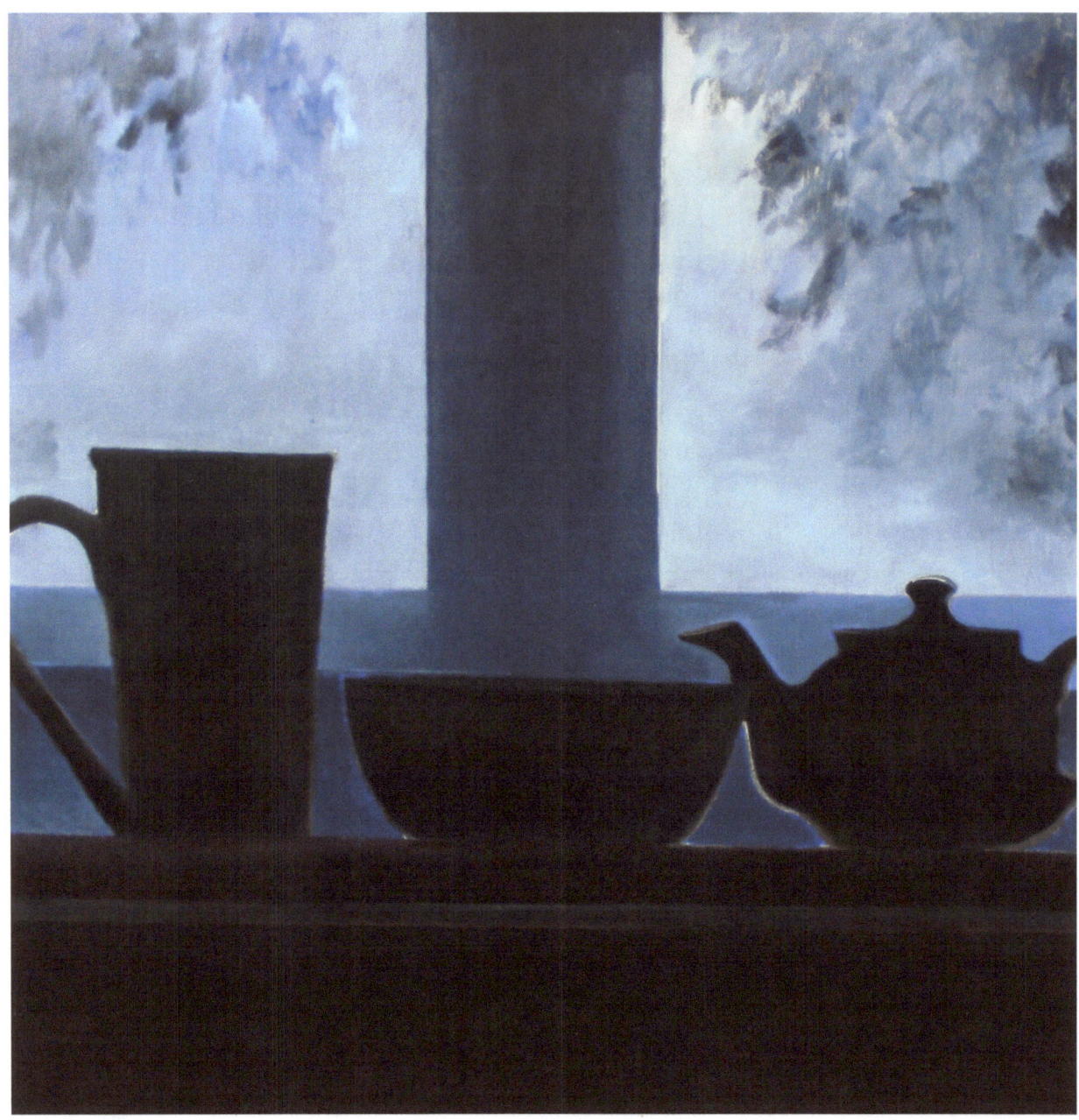

For a long time after the abortion it was just a case of carrying on as usual and saying nothing of it between ourselves. She acted as if it was of no consequence except for having a very brief cry a few hours after the procedure when she admitted she did not know what she had really done. For the next several months that we stayed together it wasn't mentioned, not by me and not by her. Nevertheless it was like an elephant in the sitting room the whole time.

BREAKFAST FOR ONE

Leading up to the abortion it was all about her house, the recent move, and her being between jobs. After the termination she said, "let's wait until I'm back in work for six months and we'll try again for a baby", but also making sure her contraceptives were in place this time.

She ignored completely that I was already in work and was willing to help support her and the baby she terminated. But for someone like her who owned a Jaguar the idea of being supported by a boyfriend who drove an old Rover didn't somehow cut the mustard.

Two nights running and just days before the abortion she came to stay with me, making a 180 mile round trip each night. She was scared and was in that twilight world of wavering and indecision. She admitted she felt growing warmth towards the baby. I also felt a paternal instinct in me for the first time in my life; it felt very different from anything else I had felt and also rather natural and a satisfying feeling. I put my hand on her tummy and we both felt very close for a moment and I guess like a family should feel. I might add she also looked very beautiful and radiant, a real healthy motherly woman in her prime and it looked like motherhood suited her. But the devil had gotten into her with fear of financial insecurity and just plain self will. Against that kind of thinking I was powerless to stop her or change her mind.

I spoke to her on the morning of the abortion and found myself pleading for the baby's life. All gone now was the political correctness of it being her choice, her body, her life, it was all just raw emotion and a father's natural instinct of wanting to protect his child. She acknowledged my objection but had decided on her course of action and I had no other option but to go to work that day. Her friend came around to pick her up to take her to the Marie Stopes clinic in Cambridge. They advised that she bring someone with her as she would not be able to drive herself for at least two weeks after the procedure. She told me there were anti-abortion protesters outside the clinic; she had to pass by them and it was distressing. She said the clinic staff left her in a room alone for an hour before the procedure and she began to panic and called me. I told her to get up and leave. She was wavering at that point but then the moment passed and she resolved to go through with it. I tried calling again but the phone went into answer-phone so when I got back from work later that day I called her up but it was all over with. She was already back home. I naturally got angry again with her over the phone and she reminded me I had offered to support her decision. She tried lame excuses to put me off coming to see her but I drove up anyway. When I got there she looked sheepish but unrepentant; she said she felt fine about it. She commented that all the morning sickness and nausea had left her immediately once the baby had been removed from her womb. I lost my temper again and said; "How could you let those ghouls with their face masks on, those bastards, do such a thing to you?" She got upset at my reaction and I backed off.

I quickly calmed down when I realized my behaviour had upset her and thus began my time of supporting her decision to terminate. She later admitted it was a mistake, and, would never ever go through it again; that we must plan for another baby as if we could summon one up on demand at our age.

For several months the relationship seemed to be working out and we were loving and talked of buying a house together and even driving off to Gretna Green to get married and I even bought a ring which I kept back waiting for the right moment to propose. But then she returned to work and afterwards it became rather a one sided relationship, as she took on the corporate and boardroom executive role again and we lost that loving feeling and sparkle we had tried hard to kindle.

My father had died in late March and she fell pregnant in autumn – her first time and mine too. We were both in our forties and it was a shock for both of us. A month after the abortion I travelled to India on a pre-arranged Pilgrimage to make merit for my recently deceased father. I wanted to gaze on and pray

BREAKFAST FOR ONE

beside the river Ganges, that mighty life blood of India and the flowing water that fed all of ancient Indian wisdom; the life and wealth of the great Indus Valley Civilization.

The ultimate source of the Ganges is high up in the Himalayas and the river had brought untold riches from the land of snows to build up the great sub-continent's civilizations for thousands of years and was the source of her wealth, feeding countless millions as the greatest South Asian country's food basket. I had already seen firsthand the paintings from Tibet by the Russian explorer and mystic artist Nicholas Roerich at his museum in New York some years earlier so knew of the ancient myth of Shambhala.

The Ganges was all I imagined it would be, big and wide, fast flowing and the colour of mud, denoting rich sediment, just like I remembered the River Plate in South America. I took a boat trip down the Ganges and dropped a posy of flowers with a lighted candle inside as an offering to the river gods. I watched the candle flicker as it floated away towards the sea as the burning Ghats ashore lit up the night sky. The funeral pyres in Varanasi continue non-stop, twenty four hours a day. Dead people are brought by relatives from all over India to be cremated on this venerable spiritual site, the holiest place in all India. As I sat in the boat and watched the burning Ghats from offshore the baby memory was in me too somewhere resting in my mind's eye together with my father in the flowing rivers of mighty India. Now their spirits were all mixed in with the ashes of faithful Hindus and all the good spirits of ancient India who linger around here amongst the life-giving monsoon waters that come direct from the roof of the world, the mighty Himalayas.

The painting called 'Breakfast for One' reflects my life as it is now and since we split up. I sit alone each morning at breakfast and bury my loneliness in the morning ritual of coffee, cereal, tea and toast and my ex-partner I guess is doing the same, at least the last time I saw her. Now when we occasionally do meet, we pass each other in the street like strangers with barely an uncomfortable second glance. Both of us hurrying by and trying to get away from the guilty secret we now hold together and the short blessed memory of that foetus we terminated.

Because in our two hearts the baby still beats like some unwanted abortion song playing non-stop on the Jukebox which never gets tired of giving playback to couples caught in a jam who take the easy way out. For the unsuspecting, beware the abortion hit song has a tempo of 100 bmp (beats per minute), 6000 beats per hour, 144,000 beats per day and times that by two hearts and you will have 288,000 beats of grief all day long between you. Then times it by a week and you will have 2,016,000 beats of heartburn and by year's end you will have clocked up 104,832,000 grief beats per calendar year and since the deed was done in our little Greek tragedy it's now 419,328,000 beats of heartache and counting.

That all adds up to non-stop chest pain and eventually your heart will just break and you will cry out to God for His mercy. But just in case AWOL parents believe they can run away or lose each other and then find another lover to escape their baby's heartbeat, think again. Just try exerting yourself by running and see how fast your heart beat will increase the faster you run.

If you try for the opposite approach and slow your life down to a crawl by shutting yourself away in a darkened room it will just continue at slightly slower beats per minute but still enough to render you incapable of living, even without distractions of speed dating. You will still be alive but this time in heart breaking slow motion and melancholic living colour. So there is no escape once the Trinity of Hearts, that natural family bond of a Mother, Father and Child is broken by an abortion.

At that moment all ghost parents will have discovered the hard lesson learned – just what happens when a baby is let into your heart even for a song-beat because the first vital organ formed during pregnancy is a heart and it is always pumping blood just like the River Ganges is always pumping water from the Monsoon rains in the high Himalayas and fertilizing the surrounding Ganges Plain. What the Ganges does for India the heart does for the body and also the little known astral heart that invisibly links all parents with their children no matter the time or the distance in space and time.

Parents will have learned one sure lesson from parenting: that babies are a gift from God. They should be protected at all costs. The Lord of the House maintains the heart flow of blood into you via breathing oxygen and it is Him who makes your baby's heart beat too and it is Him who controls when it is time for the Trinity of Hearts to stop beating together, traditionally through the onset of natural causes. Love has always been the key to a well rounded life, but when we play God and choose an abortion we come away from His timing, then all sorts of unforeseen consequences unfold without our knowledge or consent, and, without it being God's will for us either. We can suddenly find that loneliness has crept into our life and we have become childless old maids and crotchety old bachelors living without a hope of anyone really caring whether we live or die.

Then eventually if you live long enough and your heart hasn't already turned to stone you will now be getting on in light years of heart-beating grief and it will only stop when your grief matches your baby's heartbreak of needing to be loved by both its parents who summoned him/her into this world. And you were not there. By then you will probably be six feet underground; *'and all the daisies will be a summer tread above you and there will be no one around to come and say an Ave Maria, there, for you'.* ∎

ANNIVERSARY BOUQUET

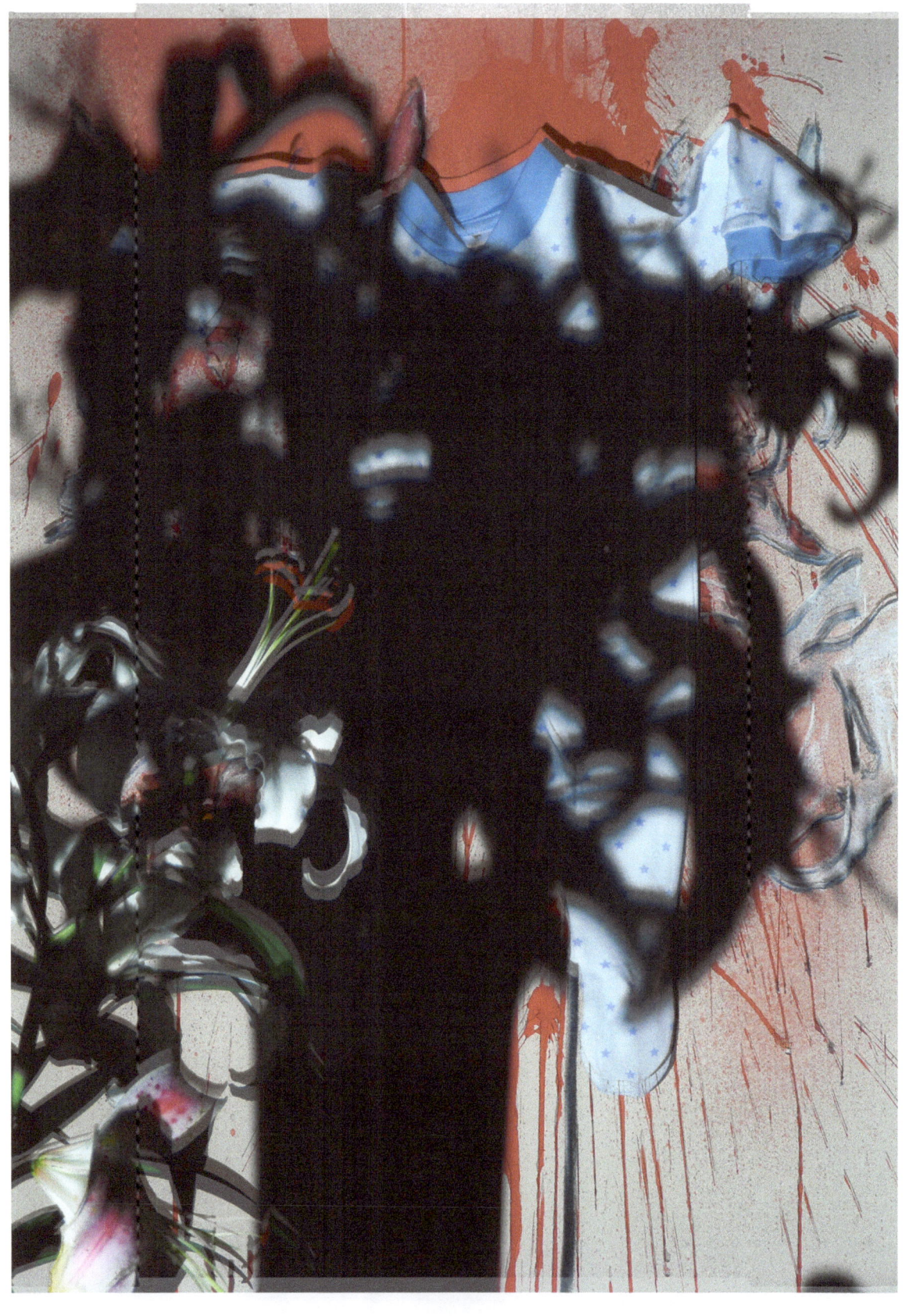

ANNIVERSARY BOUQUET

Destroying a baby's life by means of an abortion, whether it was each parent's desired wish or not, cannot be the end of the parent/child relationship but only another kind of beginning because the umbilical cord is the greatest knit knot on this side of heaven. Childcare and maintenance bills still have to be paid but on vastly different terms than expected. Parents have to take on specialized second jobs, as Bell Ringers in church. The church bells ring out a sound of hope for each aborted child who always listens intently from a distant star hoping that their parents love them. The child on hearing the bell ringing will then go off to sleep until the next evening needing to hear again the sound of church bells before sleep will come. So never ask for whom the bell tolls because nobody knows except the aborted child who listens at night for their parents to ring them to sleep. Each child knows its own parents' tubular sound. If you listen closely each night with an ear to the heavens, you will hear them, all the abortion bells under the stars are ringing out across the universe with their lullabies of love to their terminated babies getting them off to sleep from afar.

After a period of time the Bell Ringing will get into the blood, acting as an echo chamber filling up the memory of post abortion parents. Over the years the sound of ringing bells will gradually be increasing in the ears the older you get and it will become a kind of post abortion tinnitus. This is a remixed version of Harpies' tubular bells and will eventually end during old age in a crescendo of sound filling the ears with bitter emotions of remorse and regret.

Meanwhile in a parent's mind certain things can trigger the phenomenon of what is known as an abortion aftershock. Setting off alarm bells in the heart, much like cue cravings do for an addict. The sight of a family out for a stroll, pushing a pram on a sunny afternoon can do it; so can seeing a pregnant woman in full bloom or a look of joy on a child's face. Any one of a hundred other common sights can set off the Abortion Remorse Orchestra going off in the heart. The musicians always play the same tune; the death knell. The music feeds the already existing feelings of uncomfortable itchy guilt.

Post abortion parents have no control of this emotive memory syndrome; it can come on them at any time.

This phenomenon of post remembrance syndrome for almost mothers and fathers is very galling and unsettling. Buyer beware: the condition is caught by loosely going about your business choosing abortions as an option for an unplanned/unwanted pregnancy.

The parents/child relationship is second only in importance to our relationship to God who dwells deep down within us and is the place where we go to for spiritual renewal and protection. In our astral bodies we carry a mind oriented soul, a God print, and it is during the 9 months gestation period of the baby-making-process that God knits the fibres of our being to our immortal souls as lovingly as any granny knits a shawl.

During the many pregnancies happening each year the Creator is also a matchmaker and makes a soul mate for each of us beginning at conception and this other soul, though not exactly the same as us, is our other half and goes to make up the jigsaw of life. This becomes a Game of Thrones in which we scrabble around looking for the missing piece all our adult life. It may take us many years and countless lifetimes before we are ready to meet our soul mate face to face. In the meantime lessons of love are being learned and many frogs kissed before we find our real mate.

Everyone shares in Creation as the working hands of our Lord the Creator of heaven and earth. He made this World for us and on the sixth day He rested and left things unfinished so that on the seventh day he would give us our work to do which is to create and so be able to give back our created gifts to Him which is Yahweh's reward. In this way creation is left unwritten by God and left open ended and unknown even to Him, for the final chapter of creation is written not by Hosanna but by us through our own actions of love or hate.

ANNIVERSARY BOUQUET

We must ask ourselves what gifts are we bringing to our Lord's table with our heaven sent time here of three score and ten? Has our experience been God like in this shared Creation? Have we made the right decisions based on love? We are creative spirits living in a material world.

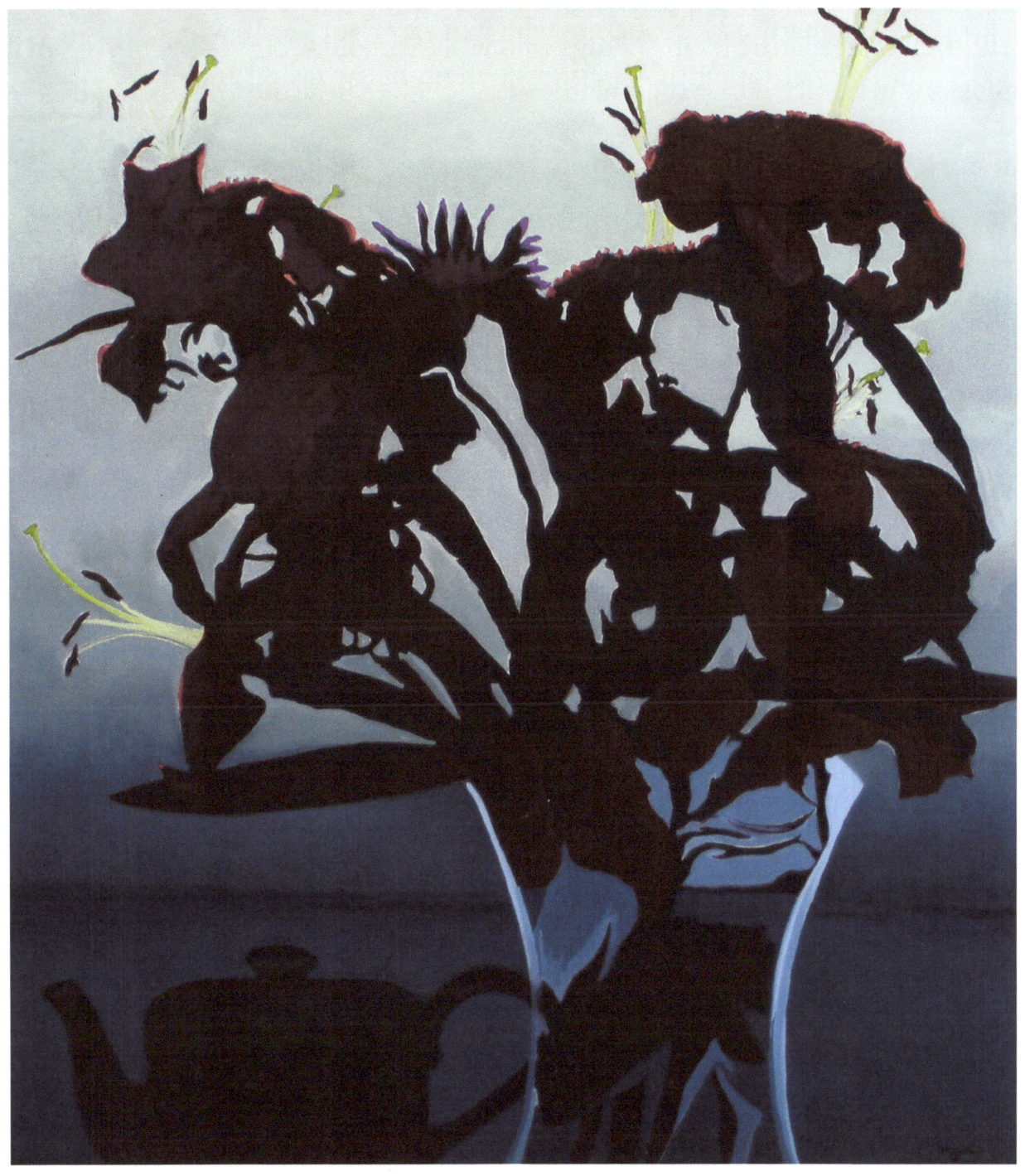

ANNIVERSARY BOUQUET

One of the greatest gifts we have to offer Him and the world is a well rounded and much loved child; one that we've lovingly looked after for twenty odd years and now will be destined to be someone else's other half, so there are now two souls matched together who will now be fully human and ready and willing to serve God. This is the important role parents bring to the Lord's table; making children to be mature loving beings who will carry out God's will on this Earth of love and service rather than being out all night carousing and kissing frogs.

When we meet our soul mate for the first time we'll know them and they us. We will unconditionally fall in love with each other and our work of lesson learning will be done. We will be free to have and raise beautiful children for the sake of love and for God. However, abortions do tend to complicate matters and makes the work of angels much harder to put things right with God and the Creation. If we happen to skip a life through being a victim of abortion the lesson of that life won't get learned and when we meet our real mate we won't be ready and they may be ready but we won't be and that's why we have broken relationships and broken hearts that won't heal and will be a lifetime of hurt and we'll always have the feeling of the one that got away and who went on to marry a frog instead of us.

Parents have a role to play here in ensuring that the baby plan for soulmates is carried out by helping the Father and His angels build families for Creative purposes. This is a Master stroke but no one can be coerced or forced into submission to make it happen. It must be through voluntary and loving acceptance of God's will. Our relationship to God is closer and more intimate than a nail is to a thumb. From the moment of Conception to full gestation we are spirit gifted and blessed with all the potential of creative life. We just have to listen to our heart for direction and ignore the story telling narrative in society of must have this and must have that first before starting a family.

The abortion is a common assault on an unborn baby, and is not a victimless

ANNIVERSARY BOUQUET
79/79

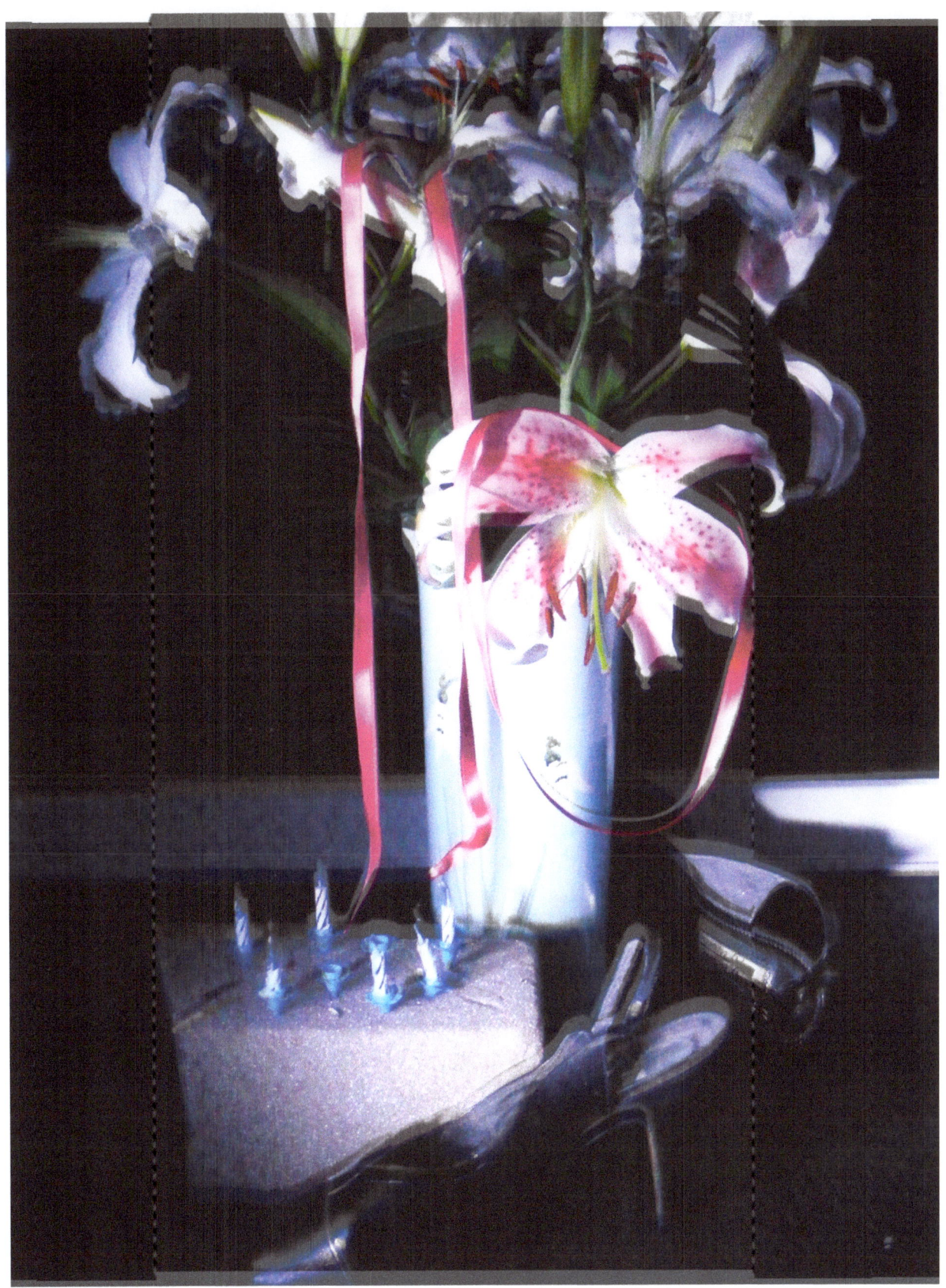

crime as portrayed by our law and order. The medical profession sanctioned procedure of termination does put an end to children's birthdays for sure. Like cancelling Christmas would do for Christ on 25th December.

Christmas is the ultimate birthday party for everyone; a time when we all need to be loved and remembered. Christmas is traditionally seen as the symbol of hope of a time when a new light or life is brought into the world, a harbinger of salvation and a real second chance for mankind, hence the new shoots seen breaking out in the "Anniversary Flowers" painting. Christmas is a magical time of joy and especially so for children and can also be a symbol for aborted babies all over the world that though their birthdays are cut out and never realised they can still be celebrated together on Christmas Day. They can share it with Little Lord Jesus and then parents and their families will sing a Carol of "Away in the Manger No Crib for a Bed". Aborted babies have lightning like brief lives that should matter to us. Why not celebrate all their potential for love by singing Carols this Christmas and putting an extra green holly leaf around the Crib on Christ's birthday and share the special day with them?

Being an unwanted baby, like the unknown soldier, is to be cut down before your prime and be forever just potential in the graveyard; that field of unfulfilled dreams. Both will never start a family or know love or let the world know what they could have been. The soldier and the aborted baby bear silent witness to the folly of violence. The unknown soldier gets remembered once a year with a poppy and a place in Westminster Abbey. Meanwhile the silent scream of abortion gets swept under the carpet by all and sundry like someone's dirty laundry.

Abortion Parents get no sense of pride and joy from a child. It's just the opposite and the start of Anniversaries nobody wants to remember, only to forget. But death will not let us forget. Remember we are made for love and God will not be mocked. Children's abortion anniversaries don't have celebrations; they are

ANNIVERSARY BOUQUET

commemorations, sombre affairs and private. Perhaps a parent walks into a church on the way to or from work or goes home for a cry, or maybe says a rosary quietly in a corner of a church, lighting a candle and this time not blowing it out like they were advised to do by the clinic, in a life ending gesture for little baby X. But parents please just let the candle burn out naturally in the light, until it is extinguished by itself in the same way God takes us all back to Him when our own candle of life is all used up. Nothing should be forced or any planned euthanasia in this departure, just a natural slipping away when called by our Lord.

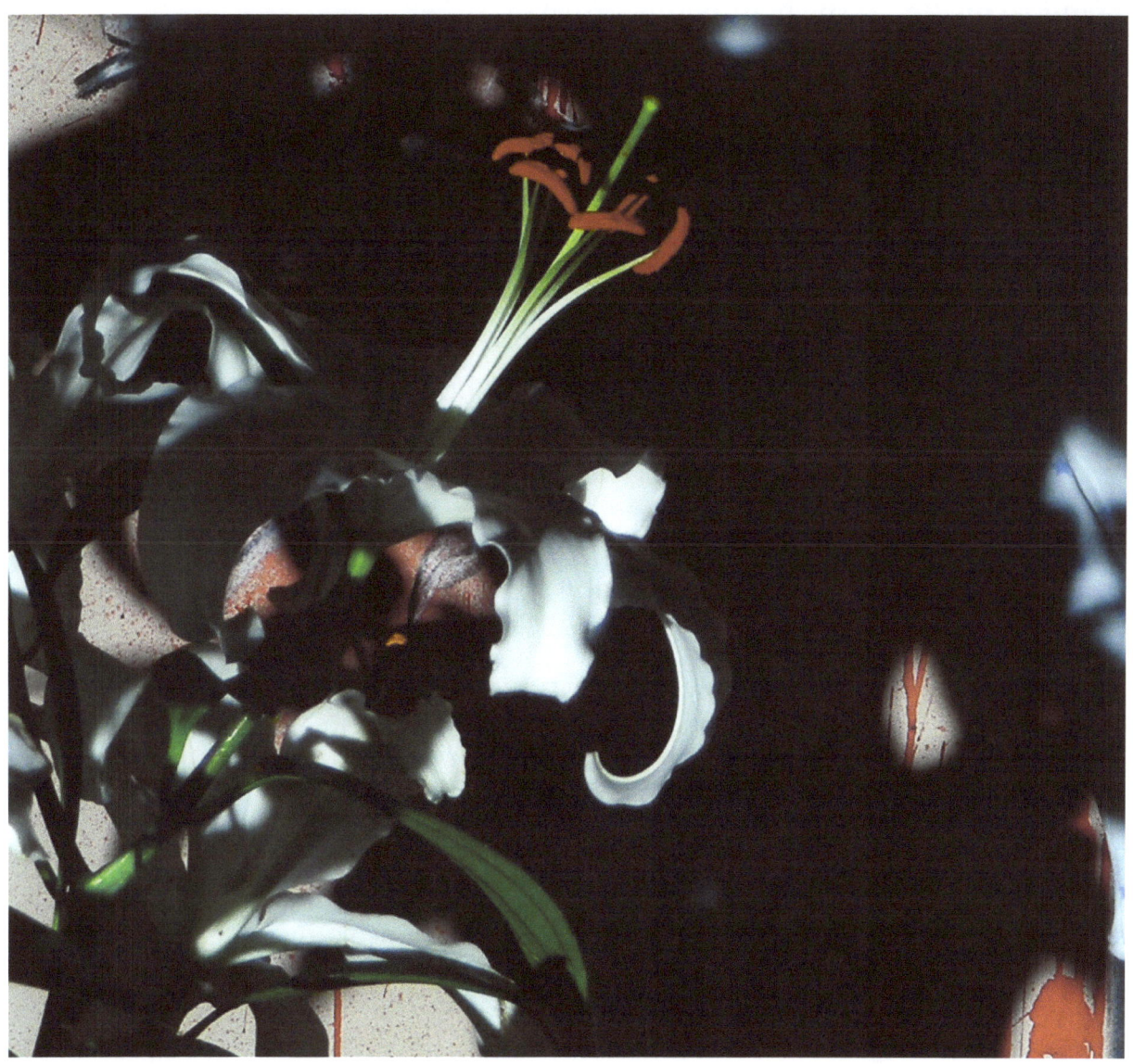

ANNIVERSARY BOUQUET

Remembering unborn babies' two non-birthdays is a singular affair of the heart shared by the two lovemaking parents and God the soul and fibre maker. There are two bouquets that are sent from Hades florist's to parents post termination. The actual termination date is always the time of the first bouquet while the other bouquet of barbed wire is the expected due date; the one given by your doctor, usually the same doctor that offers you an abortion. There is a real irony here that is often times lost because an abortion is not seen as anything out of the ordinary and I guess with the sheer number of them being carried out each day the doctor is not wrong in thinking so little of the unwanted baby's life about to die under the hammer in less than a week.

Anniversary flowers for abortions are always dead flowers. But who on earth wants to receive dead flowers and who wants to give them? No one living of course wants them but the underworld sends them out anyway on their due date or non pride day. The undertaker from Hades now takes shape, wakes up and lurches to your door with a loud knock. Working like clockwork the dead flower shop sends them out with the grim reaper who moonlights during the daytime hours delivering dead flowers that nobody wants to get and in memory of a child that nobody wanted enough to raise.

The two tangible things left over after a termination for parents are the positive pregnancy test and the scan of the baby the mother gets at the clinic before she aborts. The scan then gets emailed to a mother after the procedure and it's quite shocking seeing your own little baby resting in his/her placenta sack sucking on their thumb and oblivious to the sword of Damocles hanging over their head that Mother is soon about to let drop.

A big part of our courtship was made through sending flowers as traditional symbols of love and fidelity. It wasn't always expensive bouquets though this happened on her birthday and on Valentine's Day. But the remainder of the time it was snapping and then texting pictures of wild flowers or normal everyday

ANNIVERSARY BOUQUET

roses. I would snap close ups of any glorious looking flower and text her and she would always text me back. She received scores of them sent during the courtship and other things of beauty like families of swans on the river and she appreciated it all – or at least I thought she did. It was a long distance courtship, but no less loving, because we lived so far apart and the flowers brought us close in stakes of the heart. We also spent time in her garden when I visited, clearing brambles, branches and leaves making it all look nice and generally being domesticated.

We did think and talk of moving closer together, of buying a house and for a time it was all on the cards. But unfortunately it was all a House of Cards and it all came tumbling down like a rug pulled from under and with all my hopes and dreams for the future. That would have been all fair in love and war and I would have gotten over it. But having a baby snatched away from out of your grasp by an abortion is the last straw that broke the camel's back. No more snap texting, no flowers in bloom. Just anniversary bouquets that come round twice a year on two Zombie days.

If for some reason your relationship didn't work out the way it should have done and you had felt they were the one and then it suddenly became a car wreck and you're wondering now where it all went wrong? Well, maybe it was just a lesson for someone, somewhere, sometime that never got learned in time because of a termination and you may have just heard an abortion bell pealing out a ring of bells. So don't ask for whom the bell tolls because it has just tolled on you. ∎

WAITING

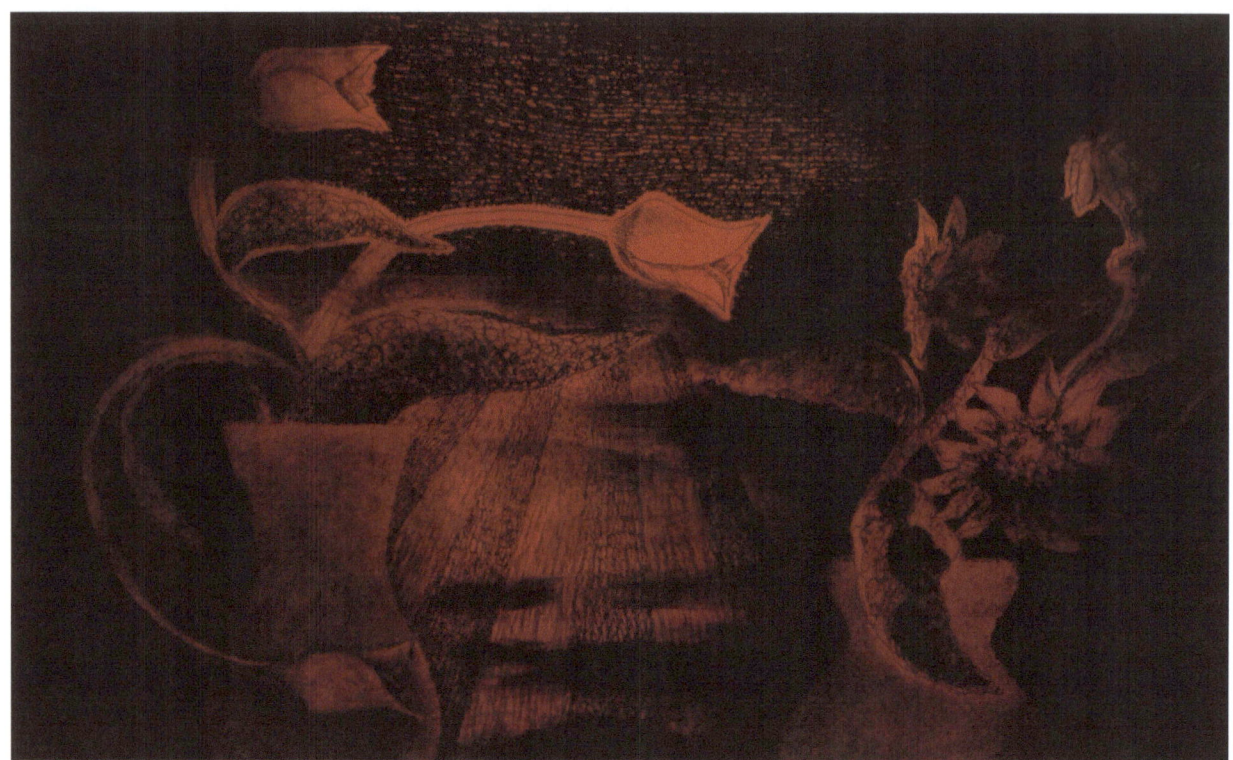

Post abortion parents who pass away childless live in a Subterranean world, shut off from the sun and what light there is is bathed in a red tea light glow. In this underground bunker are chambers shaped like the catacombs underneath old Rome. In each chamber live two Parents cooked up in an oven of a space, like two roasting broiler chickens on a spit with the heat always turned up high adding to the usual hot air that passes between them for conversation. Without natural ventilation the air in the Catacomb is stagnant and rank. In such a dank and dark climate facial features become accentuated and changes of mood grow so fixed they start to resemble the face of bitter old crimes.

But are today's parents totally to blame for choosing an abortion? The power of suggestion through the cult of individualism encourages such rash decisions. Parents are only human and subject to mistakes and without the guiding light from the forces of good that lie above us or from the protective wall of community and a solid tradition behind them then all of us are vulnerable to manipulation, suggestion and control by satanic forces.

Abortions in such vast numbers as we see today would not be possible in our society without such a decline in moral values and respect for life. But the flood gates of permissiveness, hand in hand with alcohol, have long since been opened in our age of extremes and one has to ask for whose gain?

Sinister beings are working within Society and Social Media creating colour revolutions in country after country, targeting the young and creating chaos in their wake. It would seem some grand strategy is unfolding before our very eyes that seeks to undo our potential for living in peace and drive us into a tumult, hating ourselves and the natural differences that exist between us; as evidence of this see the epidemic of self harm now happening in our schools or the real fear of Refugees swamping our lands.

This kind of distrust and self harm drives a dagger into our human heart. It destroys the potential we have for natural harmony and unity and generates fear which allows our rulers to govern us with an iron fist. The means is now there to either wipe us all out or make us into slaves. That our leaders have lost their souls is evident all around us. Just look at the madness of fracking tearing apart our earth, poisoning our water supply and the Genetically Modified crops they expect us to eat as the new Frankenstein food. One could continue ad infinitum with other suchlike examples of inhuman practices.

It has been well known for years within the science of psychology that we all have a shadow side lurking within us with the potential for wrongdoing and which needs to be understood in the context of dialectics, the good bad praxis of opposites, the bad is balanced out with our doing good tempering the evil impulse and transforming it through dialectic into progress. In such ways Nature moves creation forwards. However, if God is excluded from one's life and from decision making in society then the collective voice of an informed group conscience is not heard and this can and will have dire and unforeseen circumstances for everyone on the planet.

WAITING

We will then have the real possibility for miscreants to use evil forces for personal gain. When evil is used without the balance of good, then both polar opposites are in tumult. The opposites are peculiarly the raw material of progress, within our being, and evidently so necessary for our evolution. Critically human beings are slowly shedding their reptilian skin. Moving through this horrific phase, this accelerated period of Evolutionary change, is highly dangerous, going from masquerading devils in disguise to knights of Christ allied with the good people of the Crescent Moon; we are in a race against time in a see-saw fight of good and evil.

If progress is being held prisoner by evil, and this is indeed happening, then human development becomes diseased and one sided and therefore captive to power brokers. The available evidence suggests evolution is being held back in this manner and manipulated by the anti-Christ who needs only a perfect storm of the alignment of opportunity, chaotic circumstances and supernatural cunning in order to prevail over the world and in this way make war on our human dignity and development. This will cause untold damage and reverse the project of Human Kindness or evolution; we are at a critical crossroads in history. For this evil plan to succeed all it needs is for good men to do nothing in the face of such wickedness.

Manipulating our basic instincts through auto suggestion, brain washing, Information warfare, Propaganda and continually resurrecting some bogey man figure such as communism or now extremism to instil us all with fear, we thereby give control of our life to the State in exchange for protection from the bogeyman.

The dark forces capitalise on our weakness because we are divided and feel alone and our endless capacity to be hoodwinked and deceived by bandits in suits. The objective is to control our minds using the dark arts of the latest psychological insights allied with technology to plant divisive old ideas, of divide and rule, like nationalism and sectarian religion, all favourable to Power, and that will

WAITING

reign uncritically in our sub-conscious. Allowing their bogus ideas to exist unchallenged in our minds; their ideas being unsympathetic to the common good = and they are very close to succeeding in overflowing our collective psyche with a Hive Mind of badness realised and primed through social media that threatens to break out in all directions of society at once and completely dismantle the 2000 year old legacy of the Body of Christ, our Mother Church and in the process destroy Western Civilization from the inside.

The Anti-Christ as foretold in scripture in the Book of Revelations behaves like a global super powerful Hegemonic on steroids, rich in hubris who is given free rein by craven vassals who are forced to worship his exceptionalism and he grows fitter and stronger each day that the weak roll over before him. The Hegemonic seeks to fester corruption through addiction and pollute our lives with pornography, destroy our family values with poverty, our environment with destruction and sever our very souls so we are deaf, dumb and blind to truth and become disconnected from God and then finally deliver the coup de grace and force us to take the lives of our children through abortion. Why all this madness and mayhem because the Anti-Christ has made a pact with the devil and craves total power as a vampire craves blood. Nothing good will come from his craven, corrupted soul and with nothing to live for in society except self. The sky is the limit for parsimony in our five eyes surveillance society.

Pity the victims of the anti-Christ and please find forgiveness in your heart for the poor unsuspecting parents who made a mistake about values and fell for the lie of abortion. The result on the soul is written large on the face of parents, living in the Catacombs; the thin pinched lips of old dad come to the fore and resemble a scowl and the fishwife eyes of old mum resemble a shrew staring back from the gloom. They constantly shout and bicker at each other. Once discord is sown by evil forces, the parents soon resemble in character the seaside puppets of a Punch and Judy show. All because mum and dad did not know they were being manipulated by a master puppeteer for an experiment planned on a world wide scale of social engineering called Globalization.

The parents live together in perpetual heartache and torment like someone suffering with gout who has no medication to ease the pain. Childless parents who choose to have an abortion have no memories to soothe or sustain them as they grow old alone together. For most of all what is missing is the brightness of a child and the family life that would have made good their approaching old age. All because they never fulfilled their basic duty of producing the next generation; they will live alone, living an unnatural half life with no children or grandchildren to make them laugh or even make them cry.

The parents' one slim hope is that one day their aborted child will reassemble and come back from the grave or come back from some new life on a star beyond our Milky Way and whisk them off to a smart new nursing home and maybe even live close by and want to come and visit them. But until that day arrives they will live together all alone without children and they will groan and moan their half life away. They will always be at each other's throat and are pure caricature of one another and their destiny will be to live like Punch and Judy, their alter egos. While real families on holiday and out strolling along the seafront of an early evening will stop for a while eating fish and chips and be entertained by the two of them in an old fashioned assault and battery showing daily on the seaside promenade.

In the painting one jar is left empty of flowers. This is a reminder their child will never come back to them because of their decision to abort. Granted God knows there are many reasons couples have that even the angels would tremble to deny their right to decide. However, God tempers the wind to the shorn lamb and through His infinite mercy and wisdom knows there are always circumstances of mitigation and through His justice, and guided by holy loving reason, forgiveness will follow.

WAITING

The Angels will find a way to help parents to love again and so find a way out of the twilight world of purgatory. Redemption begins with the love of a child, through children's prayers offered up to heaven alongside the contrition and genuine sorrow that each parent will feel when coming to their sober senses in the Catacombs of purgatory.

The Angels of the Lord, moved by the innocent prayers of children, take pity on poor wayward parents and bestow on them the chance to love again, if not a child then each other. Through divine alchemy Punch and Judy will be transformed into Romeo and Juliet, the tragic young lovers of the Renaissance. Romeo and Juliet will therefore live again in the universe, set free to live without fear of their feuding families interfering with their love. But before the angelic transformation of Punch and Judy into Italian lovers, Punch and Judy will recall once more why their love child was taken away from them by their own hand. And now through an Angel's gentle touch and God's mercy they are forgiven and will stay together and fall in love anew each day.

Through their heaven sent love for each other Punch and Judy have morphed into Romeo and Juliet, transformed into balcony lovers and spirit cleansers and through their distilled love they will be whispered away by Cherubim to join other like stars of the night sky. Parents will at last find rest within their aborted baby's heart. Then all three hearts will be one glowing heart of pure love and will travel for eternity towards their home Star, now powered by three heartbeats and lighting up other dark stars by their three-dimensional love. Thus Spake Zarathustra: 'The Lord always tempers the wind to the shorn lamb'. ∎

EVIL

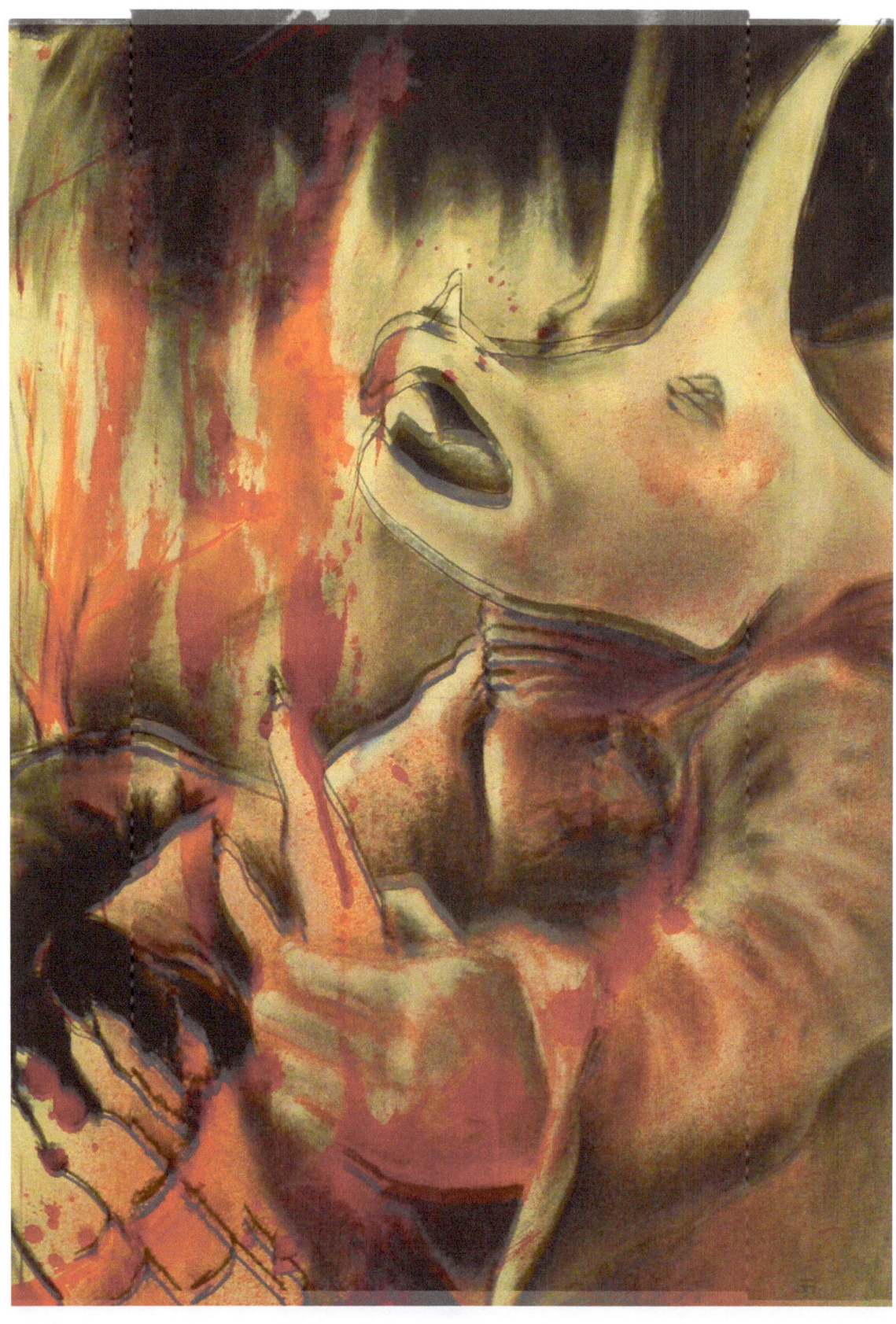

EVIL

Violence is well preserved in the collective unconscious; like some prehistoric reptile it has not evolved much in 400 million years. Frozen in the tundra of the human psyche it is dug up in each successive generation by some psychotic-scientist or demigod leader who feeds its dead meat of madness to each unsuspecting tide of humanity. In each new cycle of life it slowly thaws out its putrid seeping puss of blood lust fuelled through media lies that spill out racism, misogyny, sexism and incitement. Lies upon lies which hide the causes of poverty and war under a banner of militarism and the cult of the dead. Their message sows division and discord through promoting nationalism and sectarianism and seeks to cause strife amongst peaceful people. The aim is controlled chaos and out of chaos institute a New Order of satanic selfishness. The Propaganda machine creates an illusion that makes what is wrong appear as right and where lies are presented as truth and war is peace.

War is always a crime in the eyes of peace. Evil represents the destruction of civilization; of the rule of law, of consensus and compromise, of children's innocence, and the two pillars of community; equality and liberty, which are every free people's birthright. Countless lives are ruined through war as sovereignty and independence are lost while outside forces dictate and rule the day. The flames of war consume all and what takes generations to build – culture, history and tradition – are torn down in the blink of an eye.

The ideology of Satanism; the embodiment of selfishness that emanates from the Pentadragon's head, permeates the world like a foul smell. Breathing out hatred with a lizard's hiss. A neo-liberal ideology that believes in no God but itself and its own gratification and recognises no morals other than its own satisfaction. It uses violence to achieve its ends and hides in the shadows where it lurks and plots in secret. Like some peeping creeping Tom through the keyhole voyeur it spies on us all because it fears all. Evil withers before the light and, when exposed, shows its reptilian character with hissing fits.

EVIL

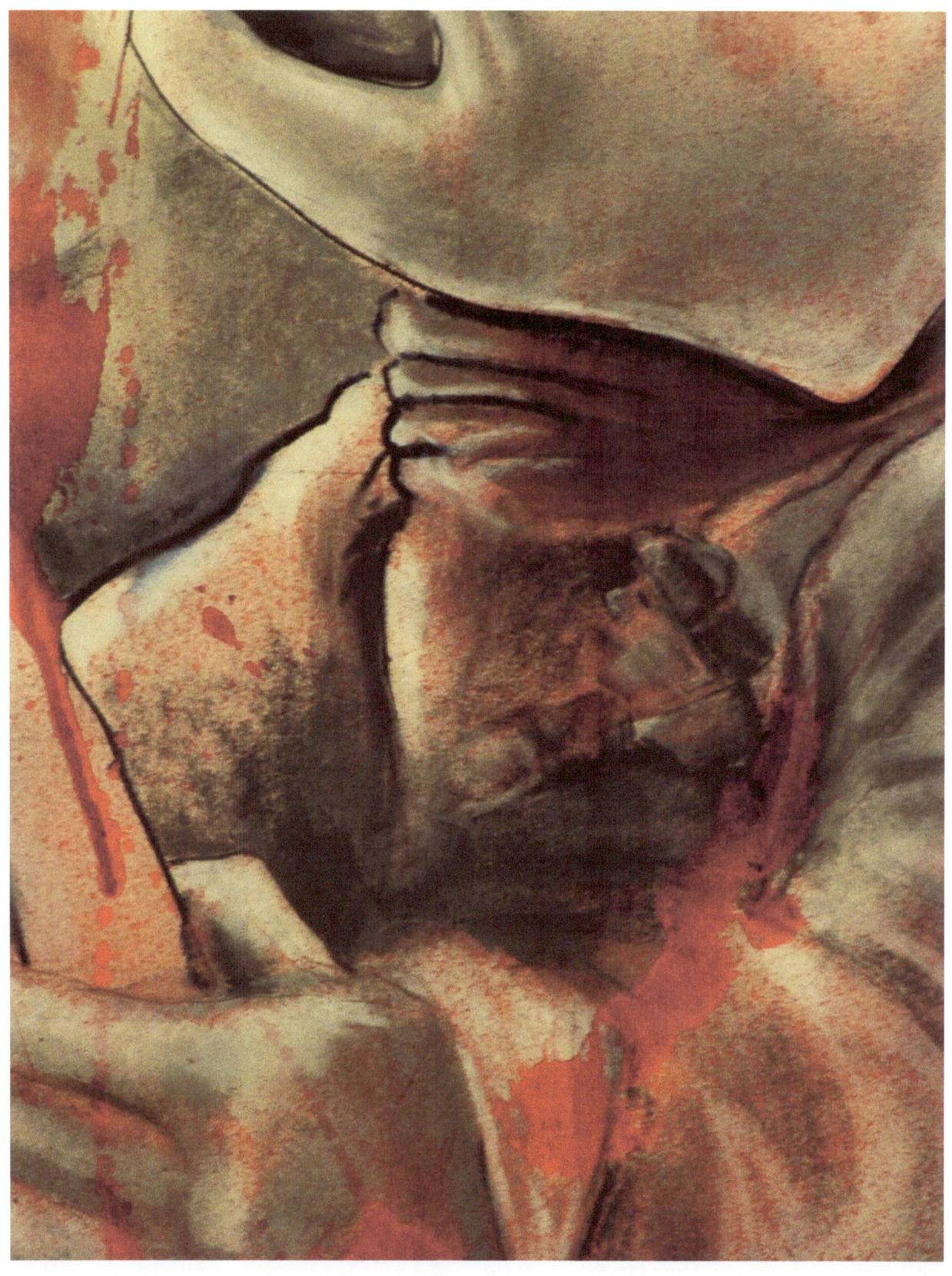

EVIL

It is prone like Count Dracula when exposed to the light to shrivel up and finally lose its power. It's an old maxim that when lies rule the world the truth becomes a dangerous subversion.

Some abortion of the soul has taken shape in the Pentadragon and out of it comes evil and hatred of humankind, of all that is decent and good about the soul of man. Much like the ancient mariner who will not die, the lizard brain starts wars, it seeks chaos and destruction on each morning tide of sinking humanity. It grows like a cancer on the soul of man and needs constant human sacrifice to go on living.

Only the heart of my heart, the golden bullet of God and the stake of Christ plunged or shot through the heart of evil will be enough for good to prevail in this world and usher in a dawn of common values and shared interests.

Look to the East where a star is born, the prophets of old told us of peace, love and understanding, so drink up their milk of human kindness. The Pentadragon's head is breathing fire and has seen it all before and doubtless will see it all again, unless and until the Christ who resides in the psyche and the Mahdi of old Jerusalem come together and place a light of reconciliation unto the world. Creation is a land where nothing is written, only future happiness. Where every man is your brother and every woman your sister. Your mother is the earth and your father is the sky and the little children are the stars at night that shine the brightest. Education of people is needed, not only of the Three Rs but through shared work, morals and history and the fruit will be peace and creativity. True Brotherhood and interdependence is the real cup we drink and community is our true being.

FAMILY LIFE

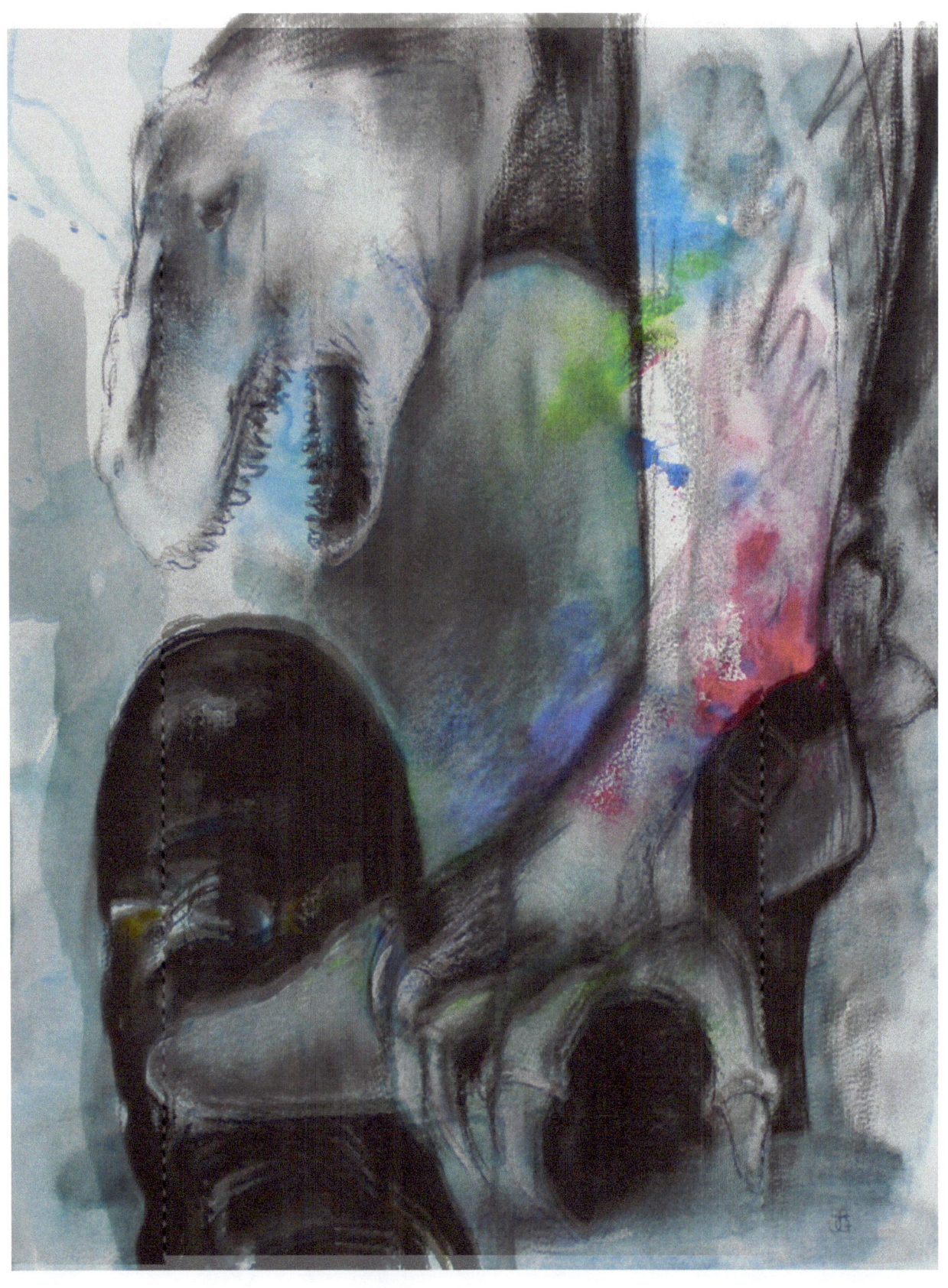

FAMILY LIFE

The family is a blessed institution; a holy sacrament that was designed by Mother Nature to be our greatest introduction to love and is therefore an important building block for any civilization worth its name. More than ever we need love, because from love stems stable families, Communities, Tribes and ultimately Nations on which our culture and language are defended. The national spirit depends on family values of sharing the best of what we have to give, our family traditions of love and service are kept alive in the home and nearly always learned first on our mother's knee. Deep roots of Family history are tied to the land, from which we spring; the land is our mother too. The earth acts like gravity and keeps our feet held firmly in the here and now on the earthen floor and with archetypal memories kept in our collective un-conscience, time capsules of shared ancestry we have with all of creation; the soil is our blood brother and with it travels the spirit breathed into us at birth by God who will be with us throughout our lives from the moment of conception, wanting and willing us to let Him into our heart. Oh Yahweh! you who want only to be our guide and to be revealed in all that you are and will ever be to us, as we breathe in and breathe out until the time comes when we breathe our last and then Mother Nature's son Jesus Christ returns us to the bosom of the Earth and of the Sky to be as particles of dust before the eye of heaven. Within our being we preserve our own unique cultural identity or national soul given to us by the mystery of heaven and earth and with it goes all the purity of heaven sent Air, whence from a sacred mountain top bellows, Our Father God breathes out deeply each day His sweet breath into the earth to oxygenate the living planet so it can breathe in and out through the nostrils of God; the forests and seas where all of life shares, as in a feast, in the spirit of love flowing out from his lungs and into our own. Holy spirit of fire and lungs into our blood You breathe your generous life giving spirit and from You who gives let no man take away.

By sowing oats of wheat and barley and with it the sap rises in the springtime when our young people will go off casting their nets a little further afield and with every intention of having offspring of their own one day, they will strengthen the genes of the family tree to make us grow strong in ligament and bone, always a good fertilizer when wanting to make up Mother Nature's child. After embrace in the way of nature our children will follow, as night follows day, and will spring out of the earth like flowing sap, to make us proud, and they will be as a mighty river of hope of which the waters of dawn will break out and merge into the sound of songbirds tweeting us to believe in the future of the One great Soul which is our true and eternal home. It is a place of union with God as He breathes His spirit into us and out of us as we come and go and stand and stare, always waiting on the seashore in anticipation of the time of his great suchness while all the time His Spirit is running towards us, all the while sending out waves of colour travelling through our bodily self with billions of light years of time coming from across the universe with all their sunbeams of amber and gold to herald His coming on chariots of fire. Oh save us until then, oh Lord we pray, from ourselves and from wicked men.

Children are precious to us like emeralds, rubies, amber and diamonds are to the eye; children, not only do they carry on the family name but they honour us too by holding the nation's hopes of the future in their hands like miners digging for gold. They will make us wealthy beyond measure if showered with love when young. In caring for children, parents are paying their debt to the past of all that has gone before, of the countless eons, between dawn and dusk which have all gone to make us who we are as the spearheads of creation, and down to the present of our current responsibilities to our neighbour and the future, the timeless journey of evolution of which we know not of what end awaits us but suspect our destination is to people the stars after our union with the creator is complete as beings now fit for purpose of loving and honouring each other and God. During the end times a society, when it finally becomes time to be judged, will be judged not by how many pounds, shillings and pence, or dollars and cents it accumulated but by how well it treated the young and the old, these messengers of God. On Judgement Day when the wheat will be separated from the chaff Questions will be asked: "Did nation states provide

FAMILY LIFE

such things as family allowances for the young and pensions for the old?" "Did they maintain all round security and well being?" "Did nations make love as an investment in the future of man as a worthy enterprise?" This barometer of family fairness which equals national feeling for peace and security is a good yardstick of any nation's spiritual health. The more our basic needs that provide our security are ignored the more sick will become the national soul and the more violence will be unleashed, first in the home where there should be love and then in society where there should be only just laws. The drawing of family life depicts the danger of violence which will follow when love is withheld. The monsters are the fibre of nightmares still hiding in us like echoes made from our distant past and which still have a hold on our soul and under exceptional circumstances surface in the brain to haunt and frighten us like children waking from nightmares. When this begins to happen for real the family will bring the collective national spirit down with it to be trodden underfoot and fully conquered because society will have given up caring and everything will be allowed in an orgy of tolerance and apathy. Nations will fall like dominoes having lost their conviction and belief in themselves and will go the way of imperial Rome and will have decayed from within, and left to be overrun by barbarians.

The drawing depicts the darker undercurrents of family life, kept at bay in more normal times but during those times in any age when security is threatened they get ready to appear in our dreams. Human beings are still evolving and are slowly changing into saints, which on Mother's Day we celebrate because every mother is potentially a saint. Through becoming parents Mother Nature forces us to shed the hard reptilian scales of selfishness, it being a throw-back in our psyche of our reptilian past of carnivores and dinosaurs; selfish beings of all get and no give. When trouble comes to a home it is thrown into turmoil either by the parents themselves or outside forces of war or financial hardship. So it starts with the hum of a long silent generator beginning to throb and glow like an orb and it lights up a moonstone furnace, drowning out the sound of songbirds in

FAMILY LIFE

the home and family. Frankenstein steps out from the distant past. In the picture a fierce cold eyed meat grinding monster opens its jaws to become a flesh eating carnivore ready to devour a family and scatter all hope of God and of security which is what children need to grow up emotionally, spiritually and mentally strong. The roar of a half forgotten prehistoric beast from our distant past grows louder in the family as the needs of children for love, stability and security are ignored. Selfish inconsiderate habits now invade the home causing turmoil and will allow the reptile, given half a chance, to grind them all back into dust. However, if the songbirds of creation, the voice of reason can be heard above the family clatter and din then there is hope. Children bring a river of hope to replenish burnt out pasture's furrowed brows; they bring new life and creativity and it is all based on colour and song. All organic matter is spirit directed and will pass through vibrations of sound, being an orchestra of assembly. The gurgling of new born babies, the happy language of dolphins crossing the bows of ships and blue whales singing in deep oceans all has a mysterious outcome on creation. A holy trinity of sound assembles matter through the power of spirit. All matter is filled with colour and will only respond to God-given light, giving up its secrets in a cacophony of rainbows colouring up the bright blue sky in shades of yellow, orange and green. Monsters from our deep past will wither away in the face of colour and sound, and women will shout for joy and children dance with glee, as if a war has unexpectedly passed them all by unscathed. Men will be steadfast and true and return to their sentinel duty of protecting the home from all danger at home and abroad.

In the eyes of God and in the conceptual world of justice Women are born equal and free and yet still live in a world which is not yet their world too. Whatever gains were made in the past, most famously in Anglo Saxon history by Emmeline Pankhurst and her jets, has been fought for in tooth and claw. It is high time for women to put the shoe on the other foot; sisters need to do it for themselves and with the example of many such women we also have Mother Mary who is at the right hand of her son Jesus in heaven. The time is

FAMILY LIFE

now here to uphold and honour the role of women, not only in the home but alongside men, their fellow human beings. When strife and fear is gripping a family and alarm bells nightly trouble a woman's dreams; when the full moon is rising in the night sky and the seashore tides are shimmering in the moonlight, a She-Wolf stirs within the mind of Eve the empress. She awakens to claim her rightful crown much like Mary Queen of Heaven or Sophia the Wisdom bearer of heaven. Though nature is raw in tooth and claw the battle of the sexes can be benign and should not seek to dominate and subdue what nature has naturally given us. Women have their roles and men too. The gender differences between males and females have been around since the beginning. Men should be men and be gentle and kind to women and not take advantage of a woman's natural physical weakness and her emotional need for love and children. Women are torch bearers of the human race and by putting the shoe on the other foot will bring much needed balance in our world and so build up a New Jerusalem here on Earth. Amen to that.

MEDITATION ON VIOLENCE

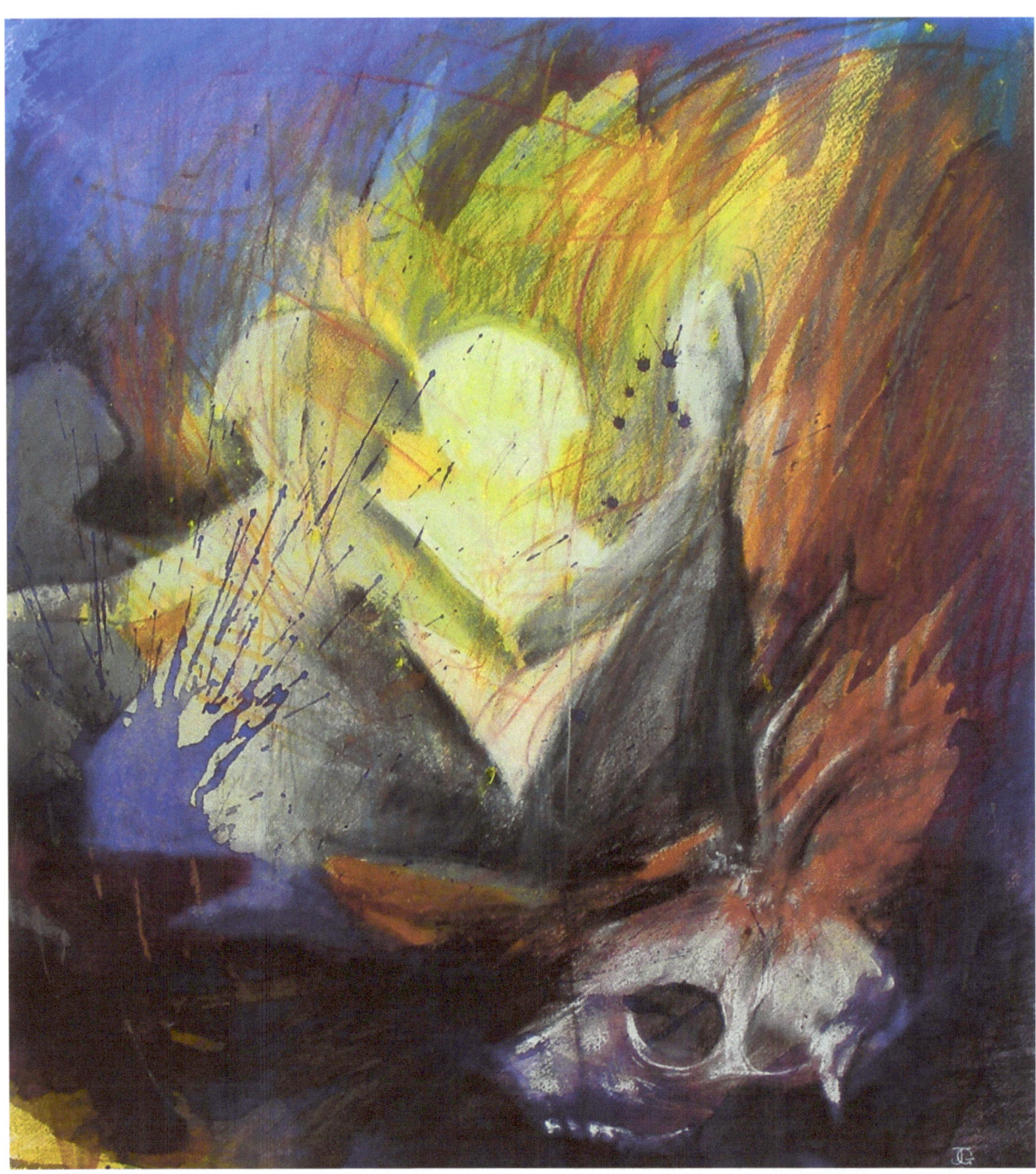

This is really a hymn that all the cut out children sing while they dance in the flames of God's eternal love. They want us to know that they love us, forgive us and pray for us. And that no created thing can separate us from God's eternal love.

MEDITATION ON VIOLENCE

Bless the Lord, all you works of the Lord;
praise and exult him above all forever.
Heavens, bless the Lord;
All you waters that are above the heavens,
bless the Lord, let all the powers bless the Lord.
Sun and moon, bless the Lord; stars of heaven, bless the Lord.
Fire and heat, dews and hoar frost,
Ice and snow, nights and days, bless the Lord.
Light and darkness, bless the Lord.
Let the earth bless the Lord; let it praise and exalt him above all forever.
All you beasts and cattle bless the Lord;
sons of men, bless the Lord.
Israel bless the Lord; praise and exalt him above all forever.
Priests of the Lord, bless the Lord; servants of the Lord, bless the Lord.
Spirits and souls of the just, bless the Lord; holy men of humble heart, bless the Lord.
Ananias, Azarias and Mizael, bless the Lord; praise and exalt him above all forever.
Blessed are you, Lord in the firmament of heaven;
and worthy of praise, and glorious above all
forever.

(Taken from Daniel, Chapter 3) ▪

List of Colour Reproductions

Page 8 "Soul Shoe" from How it all Began: mixed media on archival paper 72 x 53 cm

Page 12 "Target Blastula": mixed media on archival paper 56 x 37 cm

Page 14 "Clock and Roses" from Jonah of Nineveh: mixed media on archival paper 72 x 53 cm

Page 18 "Hammer and Flowers" from Hammer of Decision: mixed media on archival paper 72 x 53 cm

Page 20 "Hammer and Flowers II" from Hammer of Decision: mixed media on archival paper 72 x 53 cm

Page 24 "Rose Hips and the Sea": oil on gesso panel 31 x 50 cm

Page 28 "Bearing Witness": mixed media on archival paper 59 x 44 cm

Page 32 "Bearing Witness" detail

Page 36 "Stardust": mixed media on archival paper 42 x 55 cm

Page 40 "Stardust" detail

Page 42 "Children and Flowers" from Cloud Children: mixed media on archival paper 38 x 56 cm

Page 46 "Children and Flowers" detail

Page 50 "Hanging Shoes" from Palms of Our Lord: mixed media on archival paper 72 x 53 cm

Page 52 "Hanging Shoes" detail

MEDITATION ON VIOLENCE

Page 54 "Hanging Shoes" detail

Page 56 "Hanging Red Shoes" from Suicide: mixed media on archival paper 53 x 72 cm

Page 58 "Hanging Red Shoes" detail

Page 60 "Night Flowers": oil on gesso panel 61 x 45 cm

Page 62 "Night Flowers" detail

Page 64 "Sunflowers": oil on gesso panel 63 x 58 cm

Page 66 "Sunflowers" detail

Page 68 "Breakfast for One": oil on gesso panel 48 x 48 cm

Page 74 "Anniversary Bouquet": artist's photograph

Page 77 "Anniversary Bouquet": oil on gesso panel 53 x 61 cm

Page 79 "Anniversary Bouquet": artist's photograph

Page 81 "Anniversary Bouquet" detail: artist's photograph

Page 84 "Waiting": mixed media on archival paper 44 x 59 cm

Page 90 "Evil": mixed media on archival paper 73 x 52 cm

Page 92 "Evil" detail

Page 94 "Family Life": mixed media on archival paper 40 x 51 cm

Page 100 "Meditation on Violence": mixed media on archival paper 50 x 52 cm

Helplines and Contacts for anyone who has been troubled reading this book

Struggling after an abortion? You are not alone. Non-judgemental and confidential help is available.

Contact: *claire@archtrust.org.uk*

Helpline evenings 7 days a week 7pm-10pm *0845 603 8501*

Mon-Fri 9am to 5pm
Free one-to-one counselling by phoning: *0845 603 8501*

CARE
www.CARE.org

Rachel's Vineyard UK   *www.rachelsvineyard.org.uk*
St. Joseph's
20 Westgate
Wetherby, W. Yorkshire LS22 6LL
Freephone: *0800 059 9879*
or call Marene on: *07505 904 656*

FATHERHOOD FOREVER
www.fatherhoodforever.org

HELPLINES AND CONTACTS

HOPE AFTER ABORTION
www.hopeafterabortion.com

SAMARITANS
www.samaritans.org.uk
Phone: *08457 909090*

In USA

NATIONAL HOTLINE FOR ABORTION RECOVERY
Toll free: *866 482 5433*

RACHEL'S VINEYARD
Toll free: *877 467 3463*

NATIONAL SUICIDE HOPE LINE
1 800 784 2433